GUITAR *signature licks*

the best of BUDDY GUY

A STEP-BY-STEP BREAKDOWN OF HIS GUITAR STYLE AND TECHNIQUE

by DAVE RUBIN

Cover Photo by Paul Natkin/Photo Reserve
Used by Permission

ISBN 0-7935-8180-x

7777 W. BLUEMOUND RD. P.O. BOX 13819 MILWAUKEE, WI 53213

Visit Hal Leonard Online at
www.halleonard.com

Audio Credits:

Todd Greene, producer/drums
Doug Boduch, guitar
Tom McGir, bass

Recorded at
Sleepless Nights Recording Studios,
Madison, WI

Photo by Paul Natkin/Photo Reserve Used by Permission

the best of BUDDY GUY

INTRODUCTION

Almost ten years before Jimi Hendrix would electrify the rock music world with his high-voltage Voodoo blues, Buddy Guy was shocking juke joint patrons in Baton Rouge with his own brand of high- octane blues. Ironically, when Buddy's string-torturing chops and flamboyant showmanship were later revealed to crossover audiences in the late sixties, it was erroneously assumed that he was imitating Jimi! In reality, it was the other way around, as a videotape from 1968 shows Jimi crouched at Buddy's feet, tape recording his concert. When they spoke for the first time after the show, Jimi admitted that he had lifted quite a few licks from Buddy's repertoire. For his part, Buddy had been only vaguely aware of Jimi Hendrix. Now, from the vantage point of the late nineties, we can see that Buddy has clearly influenced everyone from Eric Clapton and the other British blues rockers on through to Stevie Ray Vaughan and his progeny.

George "Buddy" Guy was born to Isabel Toliver and Sam Guy on July 30, 1936, in Lettsworth, Louisiana. When rural electrification finally reached Buddy's house in 1949, his father went right out and bought a radio and record player. Hearing John Lee Hooker's "Boogie Chillen" (1948) on the radio prompted Buddy to save his money and make it his first record purchase. The song possessed him so that he used wires from the screen door of his porch in a homemade "guitar" until his father acquired an acoustic for him to bang around on. Seeing Lightnin' Slim plug in and blast out his heavily distorted swamp blues one day in front of a neighborhood store, however, galvanized his musical ambitions to perform electric blues. By 1950, a local singer called Mitchell had provided Buddy with the proper equipment and the opportunity to accompany him at weekend engagements. This in turn led to a higher-profile gig with John "Big Poppa" Tilley, a local hero who encouraged Buddy to overcome the painful shyness he exhibited in front of an audience. Starting in 1953, he began developing his wildly aggressive guitar style, complete with explosive stage theatrics. In addition, he was given the chance to play with the popular, local Gulf Coast bluesmen, including Slim Harpo (James Moore), Lightnin' Slim (Otis Hicks), and Lazy Lester (Lester Johnson). From the phonograph in his living room, he continued to receive instruction from T-Bone Walker, Lightnin' Hopkins, John Lee Hooker, Guitar Slim, and Muddy Waters.

Spurred on to make a run at a musical career in Chicago, Buddy recorded a demo tape at radio station WXOK in Baton Rouge with the assistance of DJ Ray "Diggy Do" Meadows. On May 30, 1957, "Baby, Don't You Wanna Come Home" and "The Way You Been Treatin' Me" were cut and sent off to Chess Records in the Windy City. With only minimal boogie woogie backing from brother Phil on rhythm guitar and an unknown drummer, these tracks demonstrated the exceedingly pervasive influence of B.B. King, whose revolutionary approach to electric blues guitar turned everyone around in the fifties. Despite his youthfulness and lack of sophistication, however, an unmistakable aura of energy and intensity pervaded Buddy's guitar work and vocals.

Packing his "grip" and making his "getaway," Buddy headed north to Chicago and Chess Records, only to find that the tape he sent had never made it. Finding the young guitarist lost, discouraged, and hungry in front of the 708 Club on the Southside, Muddy Waters fed him a sandwich and let him know in blunt terms that he should not give up so easily. He quickly found day work and joined saxophonist Rufus Foreman's band. Two extended engagements at the Big Squeeze Club on the Westside and Theresa's on the Southside helped him get a foothold on the Chicago blues scene. Winning a "Battle of the Blues" at the Blue Flame Club over the other young hotshots like Magic Sam, Otis Rush, and Earl Hooker established Buddy as one of their peers. Realizing that he was not yet as proficient as the others, he blew them away by resorting to a 150-foot guitar cord and outrageous showmanship in the manner of Guitar Slim.

In short order, Magic Sam brought Buddy to the recently formed Cobra Records and its subsidiary, Artistic Records. Proprietor Eli Toscano was fortunate to have former Chess employee Willie Dixon producing for him at this time. In 1958, "Sit and Cry" and "Try to Quit You Baby," with Otis Rush on guitar and Buddy just singing, were waxed and released. This initial session was followed by another, resulting in "You Sure Can Do" with Ike Turner bending the frets and "This Is the End" featuring (at last!) Buddy's B.B. King-inspired riffing. When Toscano died in 1959, his small but mighty little label went under with him.

In 1960, Otis Rush got his shot at Chess Records, and he brought Buddy over with him. The move proved to be a dead end for Otis, but Buddy went on to function as the house guitarist until 1967, backing luminaries such as Muddy Waters, Howlin' Wolf, Sonny Boy Williamson II, and Robert Nighthawk. More importantly, he was afforded the opportunity (even though Leonard Chess thought he sounded too much like B.B.) to cut an impressive string of "neo-Westside Blues" singles under his own name. Several of these titles, like "First Time I Met the Blues," "I Got My Eyes on You," "Let Me Love You Baby," "Stone Crazy," and "When My Left Eye Jumps" have gone on to become modern classics.

During his tenure at Chess, Buddy began playing and recording with late harp ace Junior Wells. Their debut album, *Hoodoo Man Blues* (1965) was a landmark that crossed over to the white college crowd and had a significant role in the sixties blues revival. The special relationship between the "blues brothers" lasted through the end of the sixties, renewing itself sporadically in the seventies, eighties, and nineties.

In 1967, Vanguard Records in New York released Buddy's first solo album, *A Man and the Blues,* to critical acclaim. Followed rapidly by the raucous and "live" *This Is Buddy Guy* (which had actually been taped in 1965) and *Hold That Plane*, it appeared that Buddy was primed for stardom. However, despite his charisma, a stage show that had him compared to Jimi Hendrix(!), and an all-star album, *Buddy Guy and Junior Wells Play the Blues* produced by Eric Clapton, it was not to be. Personal demons and the indifference of the commercial recording industry saw even the incredible intensity of *Stone Crazy* (1979) go by the boards. A series of fine albums on JSP from England (particularly *D.J. Play My Blues*) kept his name in front of a loyal group of fans, but it seemed like his time had passed. In a career filled with ironies, it took Stevie Ray Vaughan touting him as a major influence to lead to other testimonials from the likes of Eric Clapton and the eventual inking of a record contract with Silvertone Records. The resulting *Damn Right, I've Got the Blues* (1991), followed by a steady stream of hit recordings, kicked off the latest phase in Buddy's quest for the superstardom that had eluded him for so long.

Looking back from the end of the first century of blues, it would appear that Buddy Guy is the success story of the nineties. Lauded in the media and lionized by musicians, he has, like Stevie Ray, inspired a whole new generation of guitar slingers seeking to reach into their souls in order to walk the emotional highwire he traverses with ease.

FIRST TIME I MET THE BLUES

(Buddy Guy: Chess Masters)

Words and Music by Eurreal Montgomery

"First Time I Met the Blues" was captured at Buddy's first recording session for Chess, along with "Slop Around," "Broken Hearted Blues," and "I Got My Eyes on You." Over the years, it became one of his signature songs. Showing the influence (perhaps) of Ike Turner from his *Kings of Rhythm* days in the fifties, Buddy applies some wicked whammy-bar grease to the numerous fills that pepper this traditional slow blues. Though the tune does not include a solo, the electric filigree with which Buddy embellishes his vocal lines is spectacular.

Figure 1 - Intro

The two-measure intro (with pickup) features a B.B. King-type, Mixolydian mode sequence. It starts with the 5th (A), 6th (B), and root (D) notes drawn from the root position of the hybrid blues/Mixolydian mode in the key of D. Play these notes with your index, ring, and index fingers, as it will position your hand to crank down on the B (6th) and F (♭3rd) notes in measure 1 with your ring and pinky fingers. Be aware that, in this context, an F–B double stop implies a D diminished seventh chord (D–A♭–B–F) and imparts a riveting musical tension, especially when combined with the jackhammer triplets of the phrasing.

In measure 2, Buddy resolves to the root (D) of the I chord on beat 1, and the root (A) of the V chord on beat 3. With cool sophistication, however, he plays the ♭7th (G) note on beat 4 (which resolves stepwise to an F♯ in the following verse).

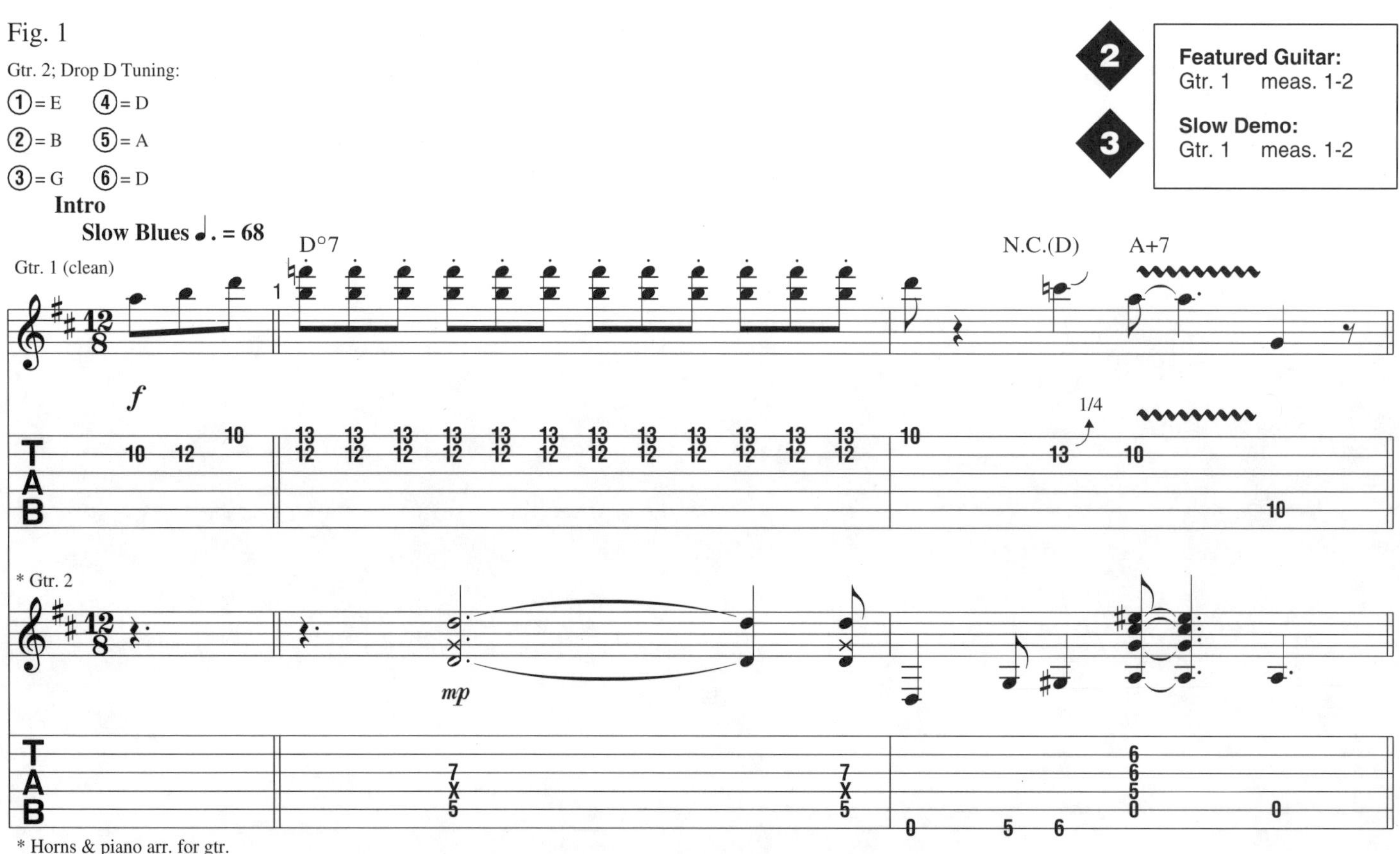

$100 BILL
(Chicago Guitar Killers)

Written by Buddy Guy

Reflecting the pop influences of "Money (That's What I Want)" and to a lesser extent, "What I'd Say," "$100 Bill" was an early attempt at recapturing the blues audience that had strayed to soul, R&B, and rock. Buddy would test the waters with this sort of material every so often throughout the sixties, but his guitar always spoke the language of the blues.

Figure 2 - Guitar Solo

The second twelve-measure chorus of Buddy's solo shows how he blends Chuck Berry-style double stops with his own, idiosyncratic phrasing. As we inspect this solo measure by measure, you will note how the subtle differences between the forms delineate the changes as Buddy plies the root position of the E basic blues scale at fret 12.

Measure 1 (I7): Like Chuck and various rockabilly artists, Buddy establishes the tonic by sliding into a 4th (E/B) interval at fret 12 with his index finger.

Measure 2 (I7): Buddy repeats the dyad from measure 1, also in the manner of Chuck Berry, who in turn was imitating the sound of the slide guitar as played by bluesmen like Elmore James. On beat 3, he adds the 9th and the 6th (F♯/C♯) as tension before resolving to the root (E). Dig the cool quarter-step bend of the ♭3rd (G) to the "blue note" (in between the ♭3rd and the 3rd). B.B. King meets rock 'n' roll head on!

Measure 3 (I7): Using his ring finger, Buddy pulls down on the C♯/A (6th and 4th) dyad at fret 14, raising it one half step to D/B♭ (♭7th and ♭5th). The bluesy harmony provided by this bend goes by quickly, but does register in one's musical subconscious. All in one motion, Buddy then releases the bend and pulls off to the tangy ♭3rd (G). Wishing to maintain the E7 tonality, he follows with the root (E) and ♭7th (D) notes, along with another smart whack on the ♭3rd.

Measure 4 (I7): With the root (E) as his center, Buddy adds in the ♭3rd (G) and B/G (5th and ♭3rd) dyad for tension. You will notice how the constant repetition of the root during measures 1–4 creates a subtle tension that releases itself in...

Measure 5 (IV7): ...the chord change to the IV (A7) chord. Here Buddy yanks down on the C♯/A (3rd and root) double stop three times, raising it a half step to D/B♭ (4th and ♭9th) before releasing it for a snappy resolution. He follows with the 5th (E) and the G/D (♭7th and 4th) dyad to goose up the tension once again.

Measure 6 (IV7): Buddy repeats the dyad bend and then slides down to the B/G (9th and ♭7th) to provide as strong a dominant tonality as is available at this fret position. The E (5th) and D (4th) notes on beat 4 lead nicely to...

Measure 7 (I7): ...the root (E) note, which Buddy swirls around with the ♭3rd (G) and ♭7th (D) notes for the duration of the measure, adding musical weight by also emphasizing the dominant tonality.

Measure 8 (I7): Buddy repeats measure 7 note for note as a way of maintaining forward motion that translates into momentum towards the V chord in measure 9.

Measure 9 (V7): Buddy uses almost exactly the same notes and forms over the V (B7) chord as he used over the IV (A7) chord in measure 6. Here, however, C♯/A bent to D/B functions as the root (B) and ♭3rd (D). B/G becomes the root and gnarly ♯5th on beats 2 and 3, while the single notes E and D act as the 4th and ♭3rd tension notes.

Measure 10 (IV7): Ratcheting up the tension yet another notch through the skillful application of repetition, Buddy allows the chord change to alter the harmony as he virtually repeats the phrasing from measure 9.

Measure 11 (I7): Buddy reigns in (barely!) the eighth-note onslaught by hanging on the root (E) for one and one half beats. He then pumps the action back up by stinging the root (E), 4th (A), and bent "blue note" (♭3rd, G, raised a quarter step, or semitone).

Measure 12 (V7): Buddy runs down the E (4th) and D (♭3rd) notes in order to justify the resolution to the root (B).

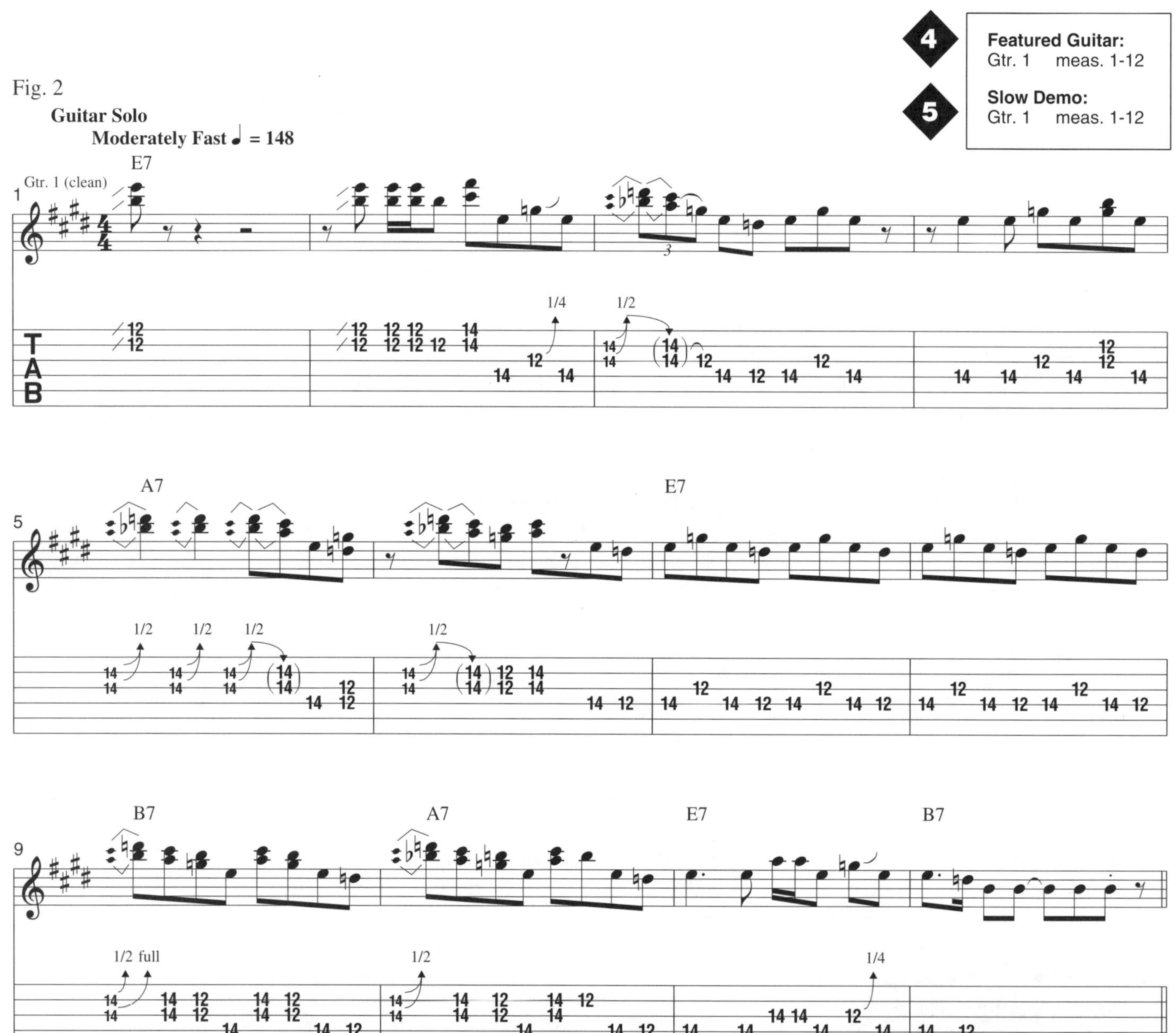

STICK AROUND
(Buddy Guy: Chess Masters)

Written by Buddy Guy

"Stick Around" is an early example of the "refined," satin-y Strat tone that Buddy would become known for in the late sixties. With the selector switch caught in the notch between pickups 1 (neck) and 2 (middle)—remember, this was long before 5-way switches—he finesses his way through the intro and two sweet solos. This exact sound would later show up in the playing of Jimi Hendrix, Eric Clapton, and Robert Cray, to name just three prominent practitioners of the art of the Stratocaster.

Figure 3 - Guitar Solo

The first solo, following the four-measure intro, spotlights Buddy's knowledgeable scale selection in navigating the I, IV, and V chord changes. Be sure to note his dramatic use of musical space.

Measure 1 (I7): Buddy enters on firm ground with the ♭7th (B♭) and the same note bent up a full step to the root (C) and vibratoed.

Measure 2 (IV7): After continuing the rests from measure 1, Buddy vigorously repeats the picking of the B♭ (4th of F) and the bend up to C (5th of F). The effect is to heighten the sense of momentum from the I to IV change. As the chord modulates mid-measure to F♯°7, Buddy works on the root position of the C blues scale (pattern 1). Against the diminished tonality, the G, F, B♭, and C notes function as the ♭9th, major 7th (!), major 3rd, and ♭5th. When heard in conjunction with the root (F♯), ♭3rd (A), 5th (C), and ♭7th (E♭) notes of the F♯°7, the combination of consonance and dissonance creates an aural vibration that wants to resolve itself to the...

Measure 3 (I7): ...root (C). After the loopy bends and ear-tweaking dissonances of measure 2, Buddy takes a musical rest of two beats before joining measures 3 and 4 with a short C blues scale phrase containing the ♭7th (B♭), 4th (F), and ♭3rd (E♭), with resolution to the...

Measure 4 (I7): ...root (C). After a brief rest, Buddy launches into a hip series of hammer-ons from the 5th (G) to the 6th (A). This usage of the 6th enjoys a lineage through B.B. King back to T-Bone Walker, and is exceedingly sweet and tasty. As opposed to the aural quiver that the ♭7th provides, the 6th is a stable, melodic note from the diatonic scale. It goes by in the blink of an eye as Buddy walks down from the 5th (G), 4th (F), and ♭3rd (E♭) to the...

Measure 5 (IV7): ...6th (D) of F. He then resolves the entire phrase to the 5th (C) with vibrato. Not wishing to linger on this "inside" note, he ends on the ♭7th (E♭, pushed up by the middle finger) bent one quarter step. Like the master of phrasing that he is, he leaves us breathless with a long rest.

Measure 6 (IV7 and #IVº7): With the diminished 7th chord before him, Buddy takes advantage of the anticipation inherent in the chord by playing the C blues scale against it. The G, B♭, and F notes tug insistently at our ears when heard over the F♯ of the chord. Meanwhile, the C, E♭, and A notes blend beautifully with their counterparts.

If you set your hand in position so that your index finger plays the G and your ring finger the A, bent one-half step, you should be able to access all the other notes down to the C (with vibrato) without moving your hand. You can then easily slide from fret 5 to fret 9 (E) on the G string with your ring finger, resolving to the...

Measure 7 (I7): ...G (5th). Buddy leaves an impressive amount of musical space after sustaining the G for almost two beats. He rests on beats 3 and 4 and...

Measure 8 (I7): ...practically the entire length of measure 8, waiting until the last triplet eighth note of beat 4 to come in. Buddy sounds the consonant G (5th) note again before...

Measure 9 (V7) ...bending the 5th (D) up a full step to the melodic 6th (E) and ending his phrase on a cool, vibratoed 9th (A). Anchoring his index finger at fret 8 and barring the E and B strings, Buddy picks his way down through the 4th (C), root (G), and ♭7th (F) notes, before repeating the root and ♭7th, ending on the root. After the dramatic rest in measures 7 and 8, dig how he comes into measure 9 (the crucial measure in a 12-bar blues due to the fact that it is the first time the V chord appears). This reverses the forward momentum of measures 1–8 and starts the descent back to the I chord and turnaround. Notice how Buddy comes in with tension, and could exit with resolution, but instead prolongs the drama by...

Measure 10 (IV7): ...climaxing over the IV chord. Zipping up to the "B.B. King box" at fret 13, he locks his index finger on the C (5th) note at fret 13 after sliding into the A (3rd) note at fret 14 with his middle finger. From this vantage point, he can reach the sweet bend of the 9th (G) to the 3rd (A) at fret 15, and shift his index finger to fret 13 on string 1 for the root (F). After nicking the 9th again, Buddy drops his hand position so that his index finger is back over the C note at fret 13 and his ring finger can bend the diatonic 6th (D) to the Mixolydian mode ♭7th (E♭). On beats 3 and 4, he basically repeats the moves from beats 1 and 2 with variation. Notice the quicksilver series of string manipulations on beat 4, where he bends the 6th to the ♭7th, releases back to the 6th, and pulls off to the 5th (C), resolving melodically and concretely to the 3rd (A) as he delineates an F dominant chord.

Measure 11 (I7 and IV7): Buddy hangs on the C (root) note at fret 13 to reinforce the I chord. He then shifts his hand down to the root position of the C blues scale at fret 8. Marching down the scale with a basic pentatonic run, he emphasizes the root (F) and 5th (C) on beat 3 before resolving to the root on beat 4.

Measure 12 (I7 and V7): All great blues guitarists have a number of ways to negotiate the I–IV–I–V changes of the turnaround, and Buddy is no exception. With his ring finger still on the F (string 3, fret 10), he reaches back to fret 8 with his index finger and pulls down to raise the E♭ (♭3rd) to E (3rd), thus establishing the major tonality of the C (I) chord change. After some "noodling" around the ♭7th (B♭), 5th (G), and 4th (F) for a little musical tension, he barres fret 8 on the B and G strings and back-pedals from the root (G) and ♭6th (E♭) down through the 4th (C), ♭3rd (B♭), root and—surprise!—ends on the bluesy, ♭7th (F).

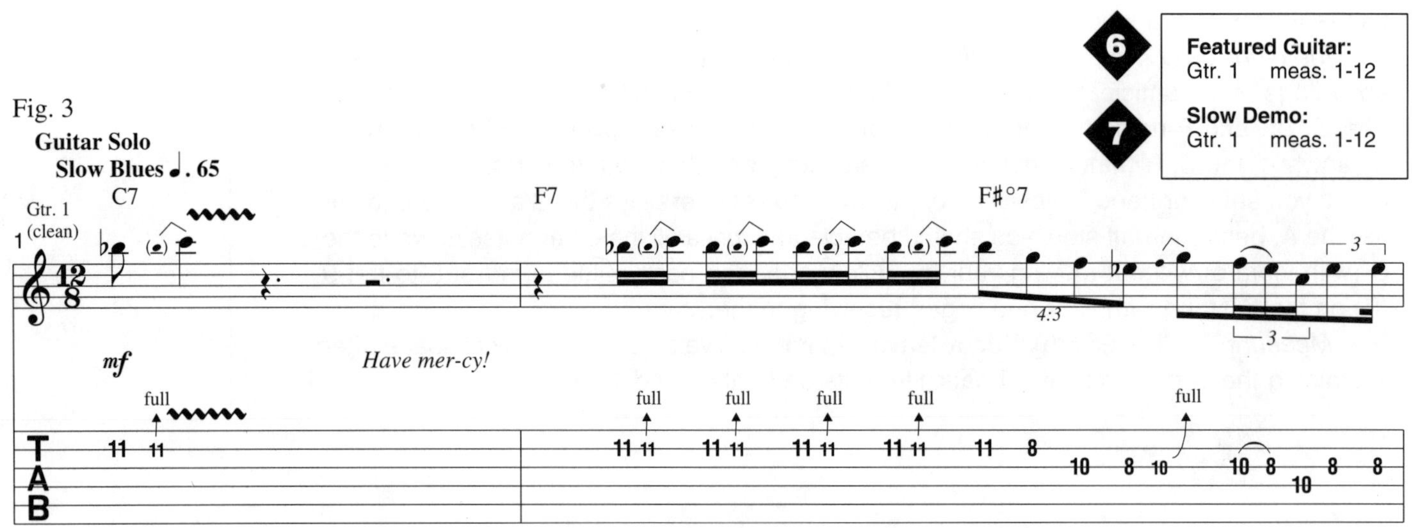

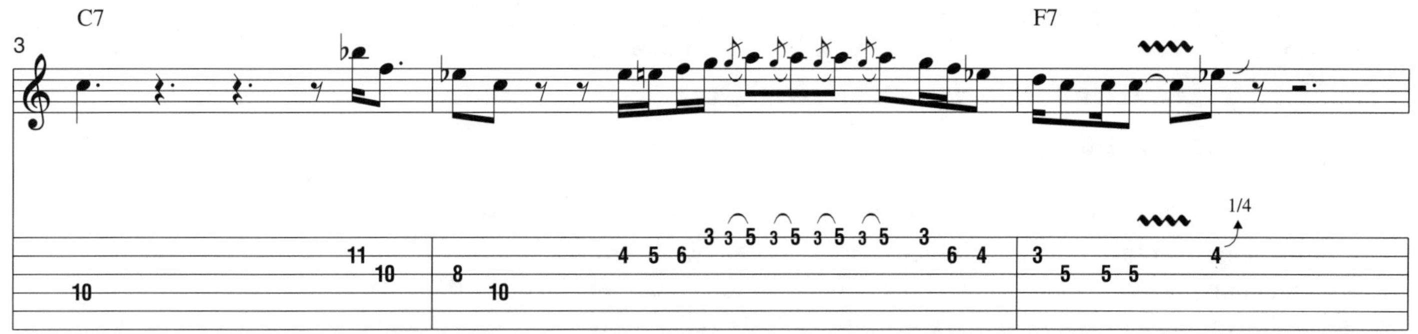

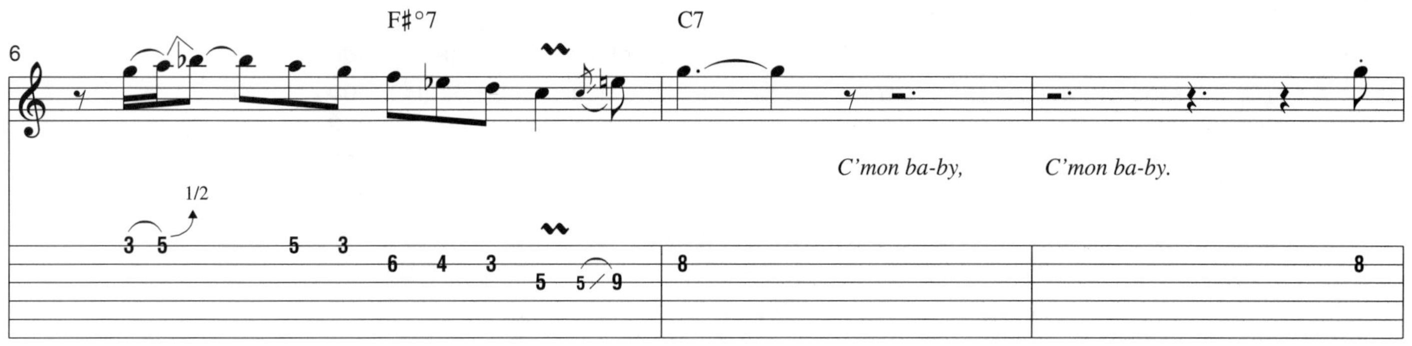

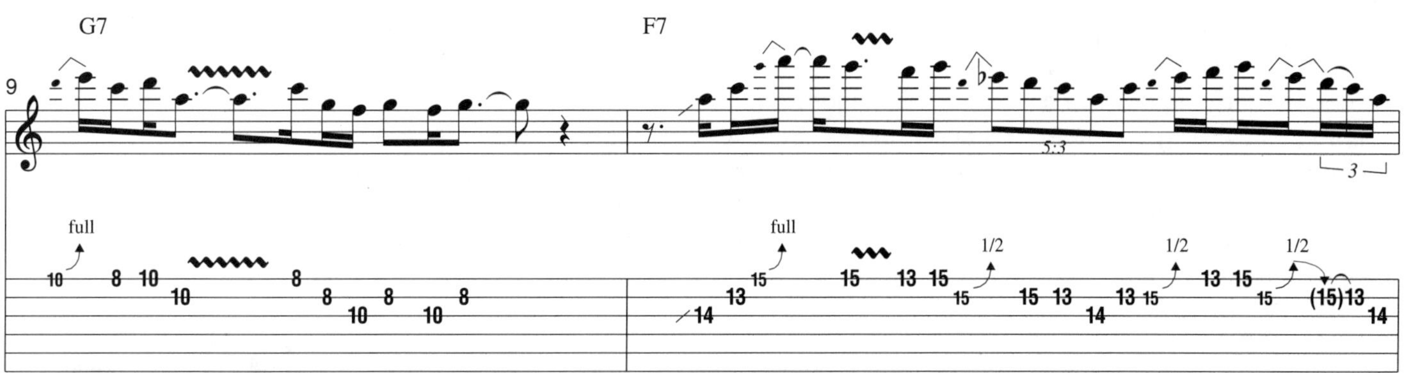

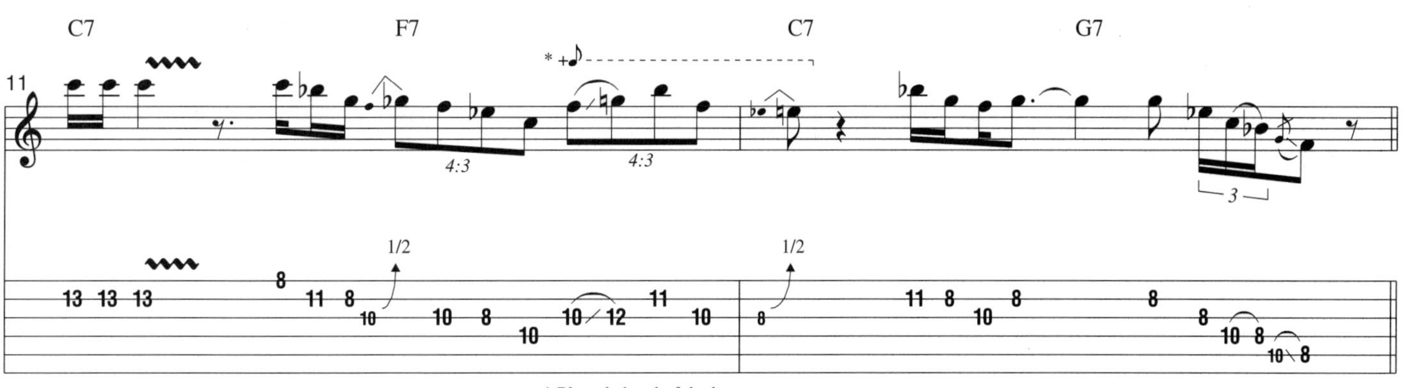

* Played ahead of the beat

LEAVE MY GIRL ALONE

(Left My Blues in San Francisco)

Words and Music by Buddy Guy

By 1965, Buddy's blues had evolved into the vanguard of the Chicago sound without (yet) absorbing any outside rock influences. Hard and edgy, "Leave My Girl Alone" crackles with an intensity that rock guitarists could only wish for. Of course, Buddy's deep blues roots are the source for his anguished vocals and prickly guitar licks. Stevie Ray Vaughan, Buddy's number one "son," recorded a fine cover of this classic in 1989 on *In Step.*

Figure 4 - Intro

The four-measure intro contains two unique double-stop phrases that have made their way into the modern blues guitar lexicon. Measures 1 and 2 consist of a double-stop hammer-on in the "Albert King box" of the B♭ blues scale. Barring fret 9 on strings 1 and 2 (D♭/A♭) with his index finger, Buddy hammers with his ring finger to the B♭ (root) note on string 2, creating a D♭/B♭ dyad. This bluesy dissonance of the root spiked with the ♭3rd is then resolved with a slide in 4ths to B♭/F at fret 6. The phrase is then repeated, with the addition of a standard blues bend of the 4th (E♭) to the ♭5th (F♭ or E) and released down to the root (B♭) in the root-position box of the B♭ blues scale. Even though no chords are indicated in the notation, the harmony implied is clearly B♭ for these two measures.

Measures 3 and 4 (a I–IV–I–V turnaround) introduce one of Buddy's signature licks. Barring the top three strings at fret 6 with his index finger, he simultaneously plucks the G and high E strings with his pick and middle finger, respectively. With his ring finger, he plays the E♭ (4th) and F♭ (♭5th) notes, employing the B♭ (root) note on string 1 at fret 6 as a "pedal" tone. Dig how he slides his ring finger from fret 8 to 9. You could also execute this maneuver with your ring and pinky fingers. Beat 4 in measure 3 ends with a semi-arpeggio of the root (B♭), ♭3rd (D♭), and root (octave) that seems to imply minor harmony. Well, it's just the blues, baby. The actual harmony provided by the band is dominant. In measure 4, Buddy resolves with a series of pull-offs within the B♭ basic blues scale that end on the 5th (F), just before the V (F) chord.

8 **Featured Guitar:** Gtr. 1 meas. 1-4

9 **Slow Demo:** Gtr. 1 meas. 1-4

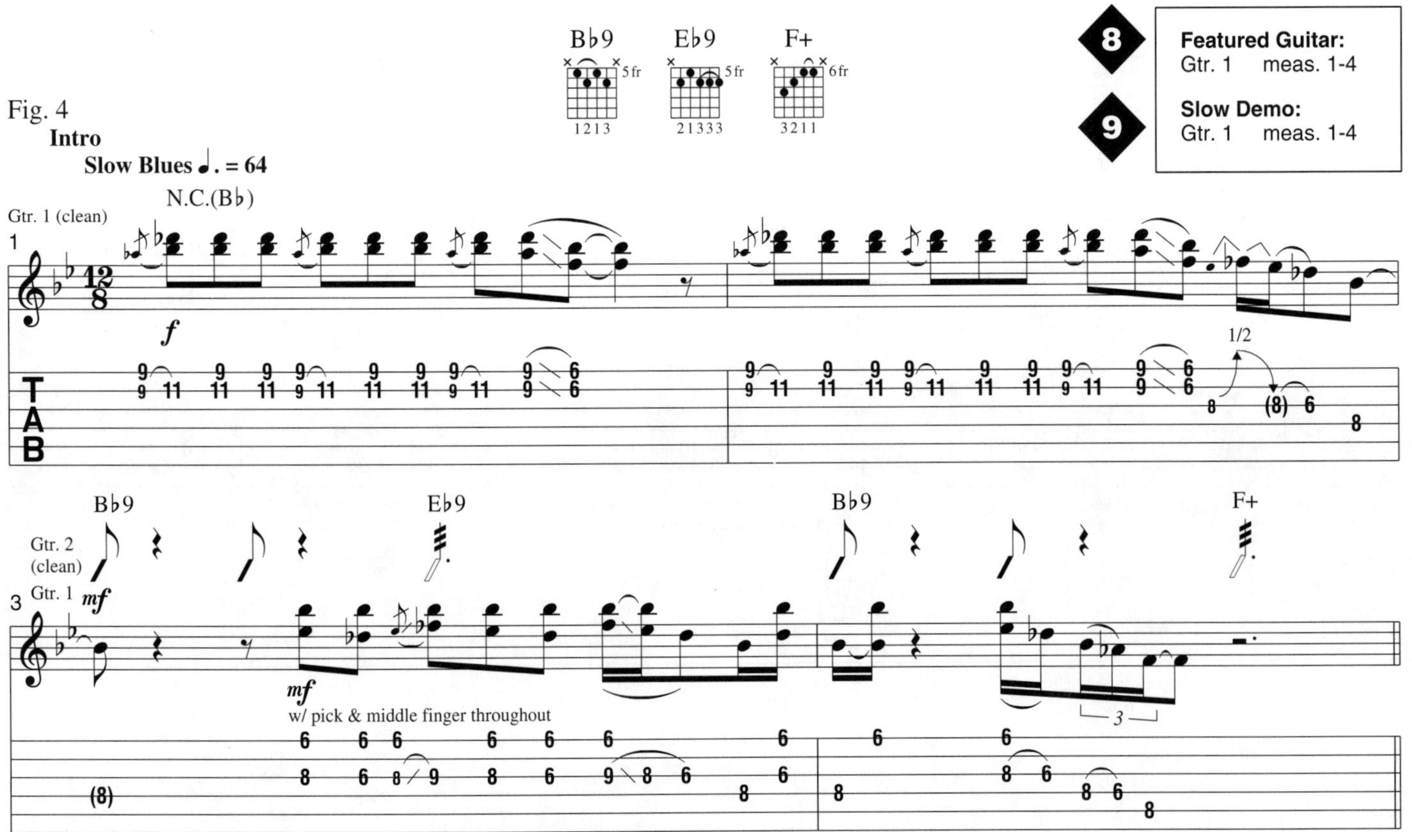

MARY HAD A LITTLE LAMB
(A Man and the Blues)

Written by Buddy Guy

Yep, Stevie Ray grabbed this nugget too, for his debut LP *Texas Flood* in 1983. Despite the nursery rhyme title, this number has a killer bass string, intro hook played by the guitar, with comp chords inserted to provide a "call and response" structure. Aspiring trio guitarists, listen up: This is a required part of the curriculum!

It should not be overlooked that one of the things Buddy proved during the sixties was that he could write great songs, as well as play and sing his butt off. Sadly, this is an attribute that is sorely lacking in contemporary blues musicians.

Figure 5 - Intro

The twelve-measure intro is a wonderful example of arranging two guitar parts to sound like one. Even though Buddy had a large ensemble (including the underrated Wayne Bennett on rhythm guitar)to back him up, he played his part as if he was still back on the West Side of Chicago with a stripped-down combo.

A probable antecedent for "Mary Had a Little Lamb" is Earl King's "Come On (Pts 1 & 2)," from 1960. This funky, New Orleans classic was subsequently covered by Jimi Hendrix and Stevie Ray.

Pickup (I): Using the bass strings from the open position of the E basic blues scale, Buddy fashions a line using the 4th (A), 5th (B), ♭7th (D), and ♭3rd (G) note to lead into...

Measure 1 (I7): ...the root (E). This is followed by dyads consisting of the 3rd (G♯) and ♭7th (D), which establish the tonality of the chord. If you play the E note with your middle finger, the G♯ could be played with your index and the D with your pinky.

Measure 2 (I7): Adhering to a pattern that he began in the first two measures, Buddy alternates measures of bass lines with measures of chordal forms. This is similar to the lick in the pickup, however there is more repetition on the 5th (B) for variety's sake. The ♭3rd (G) on beat 4 again sets up the...

Measure 3 (I7): ...resolution to the root. Virtually the same as measure 1.

Measure 4 (I7): In anticipation of the change to the IV chord in measure 5, Buddy spins a line that could be seen as the E hybrid blues/Mixolydian mode (C♯=6th, E=root, G=♭3rd, A=4th, B♭=♭5th). Of course, it resolves to the...

Measure 5 (IV7): ...A (root), which Buddy follows with a G/C♯ dyad (♭7th and 3rd) that solidifies the A7 tonality. Dig that the G/C (♭7th and ♭3rd) double stop on beat 4 is likely a mistake that he makes work!

Measure 6 (IV7): After playing the G/C♯ dyad on beat 1, Buddy duplicates the bass pattern from the pickup measure. It functions in exactly the same way, namely to set up the transition back to the...

Measure 7 (I7): ...root (E) of the I chord. The double stops that follow are identical to the ones in measures 1 and 3 of the I chord.

Measure 8 (I7): Notice that except for the pickup and measure 6, the bass lines are never repeated note-for-note. In measure 8, Buddy invents a new variation consisting of A (4th), B (5th), G (♭3rd), A, B, and D (♭7th) that moves surprisingly to...

Measure 9 (V7): ...a cool F♯ (5th) in measure 9. Comping like the pro he is, Buddy intercuts the root (B) with A/D♯ dyads (♭7th and 3rd) to nail the B7 tonality. Then, to help speed the passage to the IV chord in measure 10, he bangs on the B/F♯ (root and 5th) double stop followed by the open G/D (♯5th and ♭3rd) strings.

Measure 10 (IV7): After playing an A/E triad, Buddy intercuts the root (A) with the G/C♯ dyad from measure 5 of the IV chord. On beat 4, he plays the A triad again to add substance to the other chordal indicators, ending with the open B and G strings (9th and ♭7th) and thereby creating a descending cadence as a way to get to the…

Measure 11 (I7): ..root (E). Measure 11 is almost an exact duplicate of measures 1, 3, and 7 of the I chord, except for the upbeat of beat 4 that contains C♯/G (6th and ♭3rd) as a passing double stop leading to…

Measure 12 (I7): …D/G♯ (♭7th and 3rd) as resolution to the I7 chord.

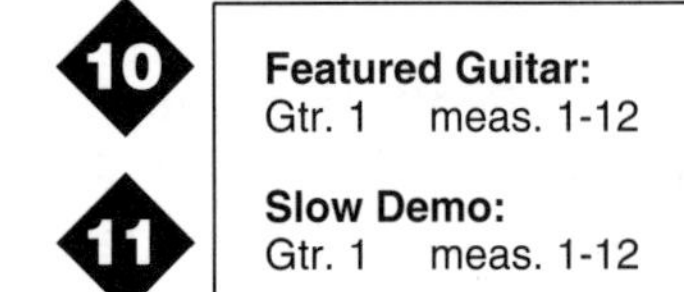

Fig. 5

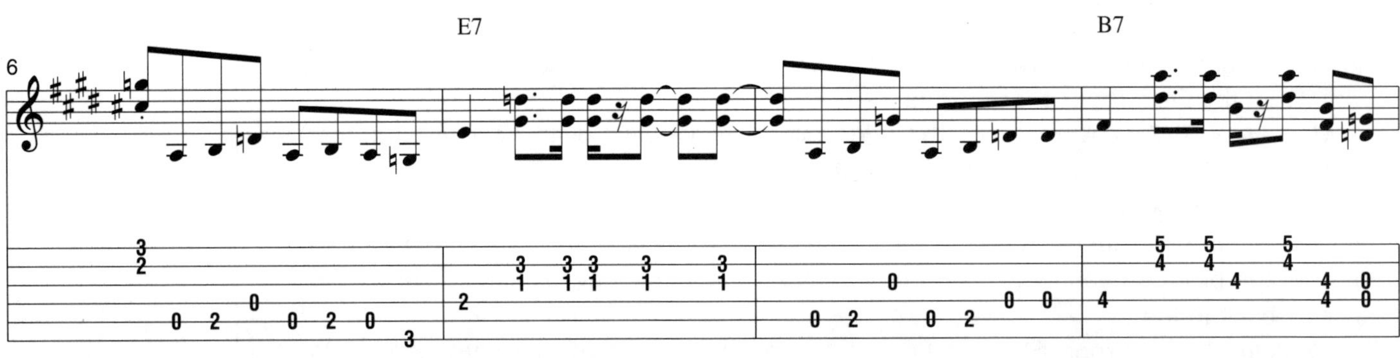

MY TIME AFTER AWHILE
(Hold That Plane)

Written by Robert L. Geddins and Ronald D. Badger

This long, slow, 12-bar blues epitomizes the languid groove that Buddy likes to wrap his vocal chords and fingers around. Though lacking a separate solo, the intro and outro, not to mention the copious fills, offer a first rate lesson in dynamics and serpentine phrasing.

Though Buddy has gotten away from horn sections on his recordings and live dates, the presence of one on this track provides a smooth foil for his exclamatory guitar licks.

Figure 6 Intro

The slinky four-measure intro, with pickup, sets the table for Buddy's tale of woe that follows.

Pickup: Starting in the second position of the B♭ blues scale (the "Albert King box"), Buddy nudges his way to the V chord in measure 1 with the B♭, D♭, and E♭ notes. Though no chord is indicated, the implication is that the pickup functions as the I (B♭) chord. Therefore, this classic intro lick contains the root, bluesy ♭3rd, and anticipatory 4th notes. Dig how the 4th leads to the...

Measure 1 (V7): ...E♭ (♭7th) being bent a whole step up to the root (F) repeatedly for two beats. On beat 3, Buddy noodles in the second position box with the E♭, D♭ (♯5th), and B♭ (4th) notes, vibratoing the B♭ for emphasis (and tension, due to the unstable nature of the suspended 4th) before glissing down the neck from the A♭ (♭3rd) note.

Measure 2 (IV7): Dropping into the root position of the B♭ Mixolydian mode, Buddy works on the G (3rd), B♭ (5th), and C (6th) notes to complement and extend the "colors" of the E♭7 chord change. Note the cool half-step bend of the C to D♭ (♭7th) and the full-step bend of C to D (major 7th!). On beat 4, he vibratoes the stable 5th (B♭) and executes a fluid bend (E♭ to F—the 9th), release (F to E♭), and pull-off (E♭ to D♭). The vibratoed B♭ is a signal for the next measure where he...

Measure 3 (I7 and IV7): ...resolves to the root (B♭). Shifting back down to fret 6, Buddy changes from the Mixolydian mode to the B♭ blues scale, where he indicates the I chord with the root (B♭), ♭7th (A♭), 5th (F), and hip ♭5th (F♭ or E) notes. He then connects the I7-to-IV7 change in the turnaround with the E♭ and D♭ notes as they act as the root and ♭7th over the IV (E♭) chord. On beat 4, Buddy rumbles around on the 4th (A♭), 9th (F), root, ♭7th, and 5th (B♭) notes. Then, thinking ahead again, he has the B♭ note do double duty as it functions as the...

Measure 4 (I7 and V7): ...vibratoed root in measure 4. Staying in the root position box, Buddy jumps off the classic 4th (E♭) to 5th (F) bend and runs down through the root (B♭) before resolving to the F (root) on beat 3 as the chord changes to the V (F). Then, in a supremely cool move, he arpeggiates a first inversion F7 chord form with the third (A), ♭7th (E♭), and root (F) notes. In four measures, Buddy says more musically than many players would in two choruses.

Like "Mary Had A Little Lamb," "My Time After Awhile" mixes in elements of R&B with the blues. The two bridges, for example, have a one-measure phrase containing the I7 (B♭7) and IV7 (E♭7) chords that vamp for seven and three measures, respectively, before releasing the tension by following the standard 12-bar changes to a satisfactory conclusion.

12 **13**

Featured Guitar:
Gtr. 1 meas. 1-4

Slow Demo:
Gtr. 1 meas. 1-4

Fig. 6

Intro

Slow Blues ♩. = 60

** F7 Eb7

Gtr. 1 (clean)

mf

full full full full full full 1/2 full full

Gtr. 2 (clean)

p

let ring

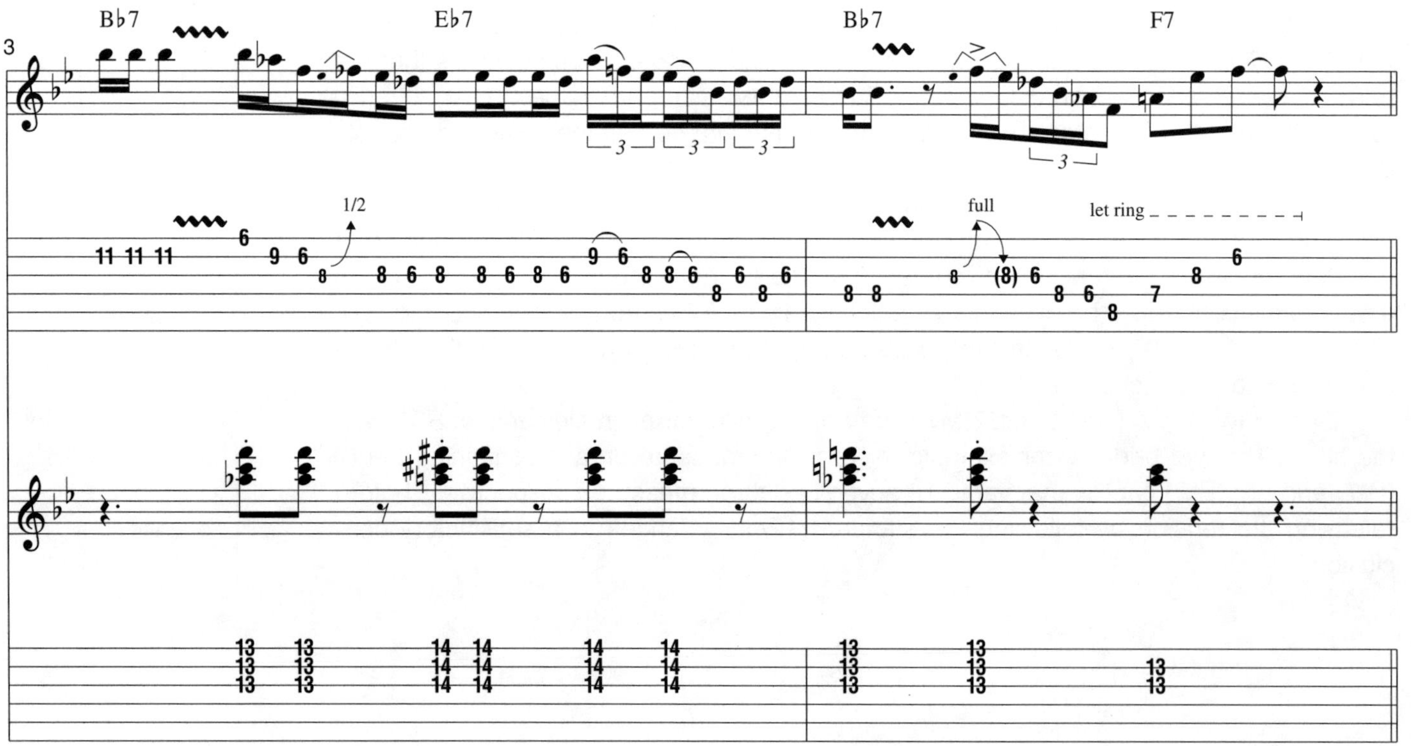

I SMELL A RAT
(Stone Crazy)
Written by Buddy Guy

Ironically, Buddy's career had reached its nadir at the same time he was recording some of his most exciting guitar playing. The music on *Stone Crazy,* originally released on the French Isabel label in 1979, would have languished if it had not been for Alligator Records in Chicago who re-released it in 1981. Despite that stroke of good fortune for Buddy, this unbelievably intense platter has never received the accolades it is due, even from guitar players.

Anyone who thinks that Stevie Ray Vaughan and his followers wrote the book on over-the-top, blues guitar pyrotechnics, need only one listen to "I Smell a Rat" to set themselves straight. Starting from the first note of this wild, 9:31 rollercoaster ride of a slow blues, Buddy just plain rips the strings off his Strat. No pretense is made of trying to be economical with his notes as he blazes his way from one end of this minor-key opus to the other. On the other hand, dynamics, pacing, and dramatic phrasing are evident throughout, separating Buddy from the lesser pretenders to his throne.

Figure 7 - Intro Solo (Third Chorus)

The third chorus of Buddy's flaming intro is a textbook of blues bends and especially worthy ofour perusal.

Measure 1 (i): Coming off of two knuckle-busting choruses, Buddy starts with a quick bend of the 4th (E) to the 5th (F♯) and rests musically for three beats while exhorting his band mates (including brother Phil on rhythm guitar) to join him as he takes them higher. Note: Buddy appears to play chorus 1 on the mellow neck pickup, chorus 2 on the funky middle pickup, and chorus 3 on the razor-sharp bridge pickup of his Strat. This procedure only serves to intensify the solo as it rockets ahead to its climax.

Measure 2 (i): Finding a home in the second position box, Buddy double-bends the B (root) and E (4th) notes a full step to C♯ (9th) and F♯ (5th) at fret 12. Following with a slippery half-step bend of the D♯ (unusual and dissonant major 3rd) to E with his middle finger, Buddy then tattoos the D (♭3rd, indicating minor tonality), B (root), and E (4th) notes. He ends this measure with a bluesy quarter-step bend of D (with his index finger) and the double-string bend of E/B that began the show. Buddy probably used his ring and middle fingers for this bend, but the pinky and ring would work just as well.

Measure 3 (i): Those double-string bends from measure 2 are juicy, and Buddy squeezes them with the kind of conviction that only comes from experiencing the pain that he sings about. Throwing himself into his work with abandon, he applies the same technique to D♯/A♯ (major 3rd and major 7th!) at fret 11 and D/A (♭3rd and ♭7th) at fret 10 while interjecting a quick D and B into the stew. On beat 4, he bends E (4th) to F♯ (5th) as he maintains the momentum into measure 4. The best way to access the double-string bends as they shift up and down the neck is to actually move your hand position, so that you are always bending with the same fingers.

Theoretically, Buddy restricts himself mainly to the B minor pentatonic scale in "I Smell a Rat." However, intuitively he goes (way) outside the parameters of this common scale to expand his expressive choices. As you can see, so far over the i chord, these include the passing tones in between frets 10 and 12 on the B and E strings.

Measure 4 (i): Buddy repeats the licks from measure 3 as a means to keep the tension screwed up tight before moving on to the iv chord. Be aware that the double-string bends are a great dynamic device when contrasted with single-note lines, as they alter one's perception of pitch and duration.

Measure 5 (iv): Proving the axiom stated in the previous measure, Buddy releases the tension engendered in the four measures of the i chord by piling on a bunch of sixteenth and thirty-second notes with some wicked vibrato thrown in for good measure (pun intended!). The notes D (♭7th), B (5th), A (4th), F♯ (9th), and E (root) extend the Em tonality of the chord change to a sophisticated Em9. As a master of dynamics, Buddy makes sure that his single-note lines breathe and pulse with musical variety by jamming eighth and thirty-second notes in the same phrase.

Measure 6 (iv): Repeating the ideas begun in measure 5, Buddy tightens his grip (pun intended again!) on the tension by demonstrating the exhilarating effect of bending the root (E) note (string 3 at fret 9) a robust two and one half steps for virtually the entire measure. Using his ring finger (backed up by his middle and index fingers) as the lever, he pushes the E all the way up to A (4th). The alternation of the root with the 4th is an excellent way to obtain tension and release. When combined with pre-bends and releases performed at regular intervals (on beats 2, 3, and 4), aural whiplash is produced, turning the perceived passage of time upside down.

Measure 7 (i): In order to maintain the headlong, forward rush of his solo, Buddy blurs the distinction between the iv and i chords at this point by continuing to wreak havoc on his poor G string. In the process, he keeps the gas on high with the 4th (E) note. Winding his way towards resolution on the i, though, he begins to vary his attack. On beat 3, he bends a full step to F♯ (5th) and one half step to F (♭5th). He then pummels the 4th (E) two times and bends the identifying ♭3rd (D) a full step back to E to ratchet the voltage back up, before beginning his descent to the root with the D note at the end of the measure.

Measure 8 (i): Ah, resolution at last as Buddy finally lands on the B (root) note with vibrato. Holding on to his place at fret 7 and wishing to confirm the B minor tonality of the change, he rips through a succession of B minor pentatonic notes, including the 5th (F♯), ♭7th (A), 4th (E), and the prime note, the ♭3rd (D). By the way, that hammer-on of the ♭3rd to the major 3rd (D♯) at the beginning of beat 2 is likely a mistake. At this blistering pace, however, it is barely noticed.

Measure 9 (v): Staying basically with the same group of notes, Buddy makes a subtle alteration that helps shift the tonality to the v (F♯m) chord. On beat 2, he combines the B (4th) with the C♯ (5th) and C♮ (♭5th as a passing note to the B). When taken as a whole with the root (F♯) and ♭3rd (A) notes that are sprinkled about, a stronger sense of the v chord change is implied. Notice how Buddy anticipates the iv (E) chord change in measure 10 by sliding from B to E at the tail end of beat 4.

Measure 10 (iv): Starting in with the root (E), Buddy wrestles with the Em tonality via a few well-chosen notes. They are the ♭7th (D), 5th (B), and 9th (F♯)—implying extension of the harmony to minor 9. By planting himself in the "Albert King box," Buddy uses his index and ring fingers to the best advantage in manipulating the notes, particularly the recurring bends on the high E string. That cool technique of bending, releasing, and pulling off in beat 2 is a staple of blues guitarists, and you should make it a prime part of your repertoire.

Measure 11 (i): Buddy remains in the second position box for one more beat as he "worries" the root (B) with his ring finger before hurtling himself down to the root position of the scale at fret 7. Once there, he gangs together sixteenth-note triplets based around the solid root, ♭7th (A), 5th (F♯), 4th (E), and ♭3rd (D) notes. Throughout "I Smell a Rat," fast and accurate right-hand picking is required along with rapid left-hand fretwork. You should know that strict, alternate down and up pickstrokes are recommended for the speedy passages, as Buddy does not pull off or hammer on very much.

The last note of the measure, the (minor) ♭3rd, resolves nicely to the…

Measure 12 (i and V7): …root (B). Combined with a fast triplet of Bs is a dizzying gliss down string 4 (with his ring finger) to F♯ (5th) at fret 4, and up to A♯ (major 7) at fret 20 on beat 1. Buddy then returns to fret 7 for a series of B minor pentatonic notes (F♯, B, A, and E) that resolve to the root (F♯) on beat 3 where the V7 chord occurs.

Bm
A♯m
A5
B5
D5
Em
D♯m
F♯m
F♯7
14
Featured Guitar:
Gtr. 1 meas. 1-12
15
Slow Demo:
Gtr. 1 meas. 1-12
Fig. 7
Intro (Third Chorus)
Slow Blues ♩. = 69
Gtr. 2 (clean)
Gtr. 1 (dist.)
Spoken: Ho, c'mon fellas now!
full
1/2
1/4
2 1/2

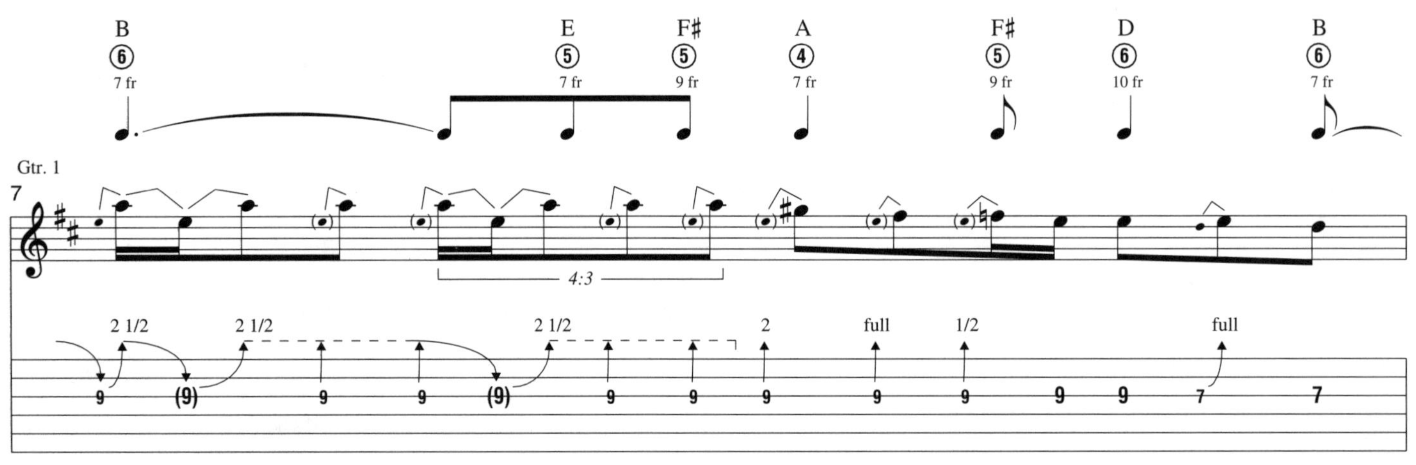
B
E
F♯
A
F♯
D
B
Gtr. 1
4:3
2 1/2
2 1/2
2 1/2
2
full
1/2
full

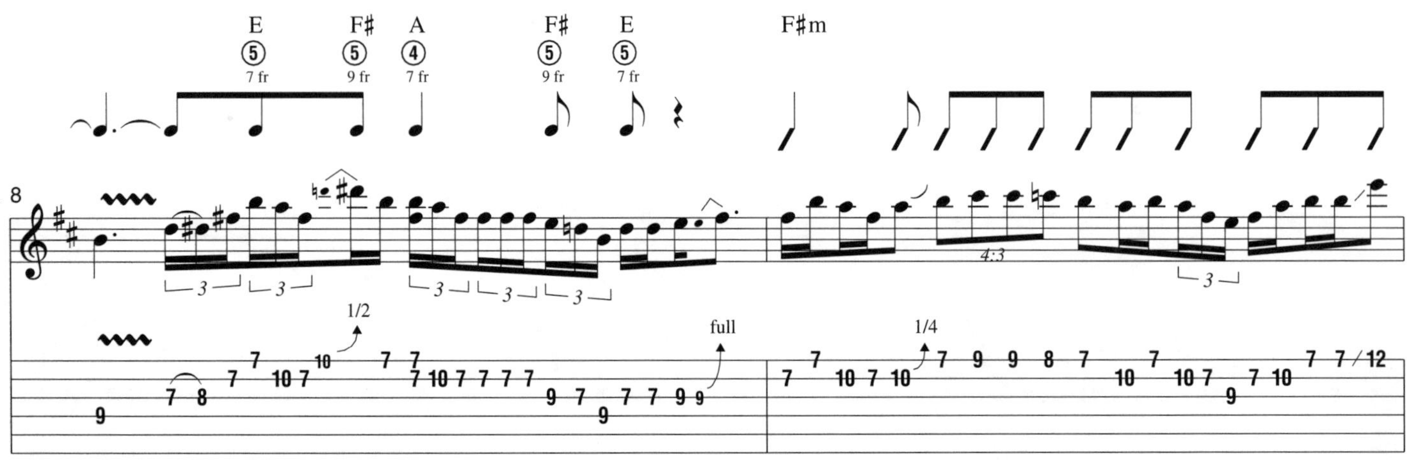
E
F♯
A
F♯
E
F♯m
4:3
1/2
full
1/4

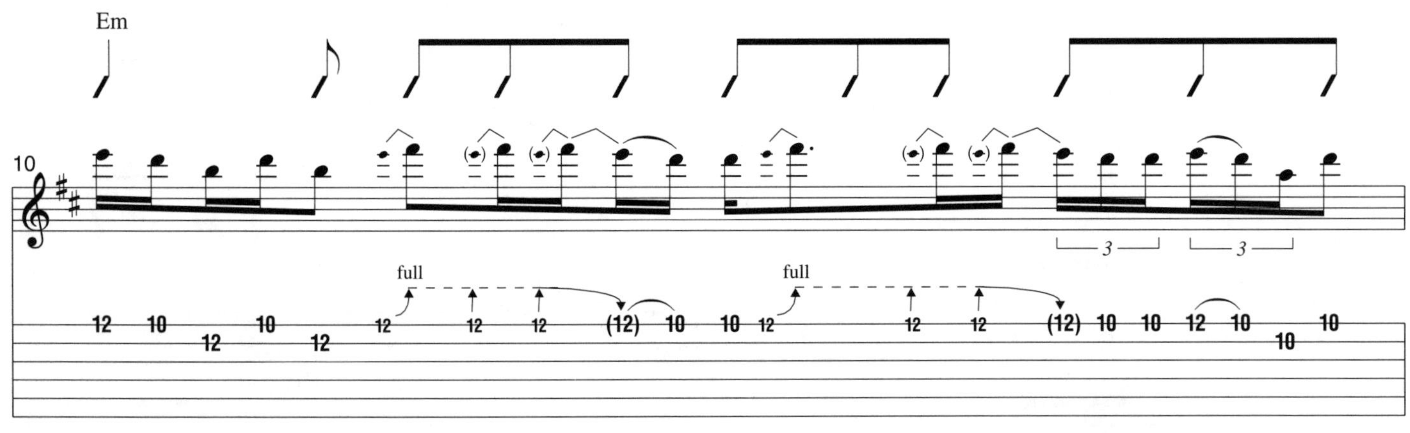
Em
full
full

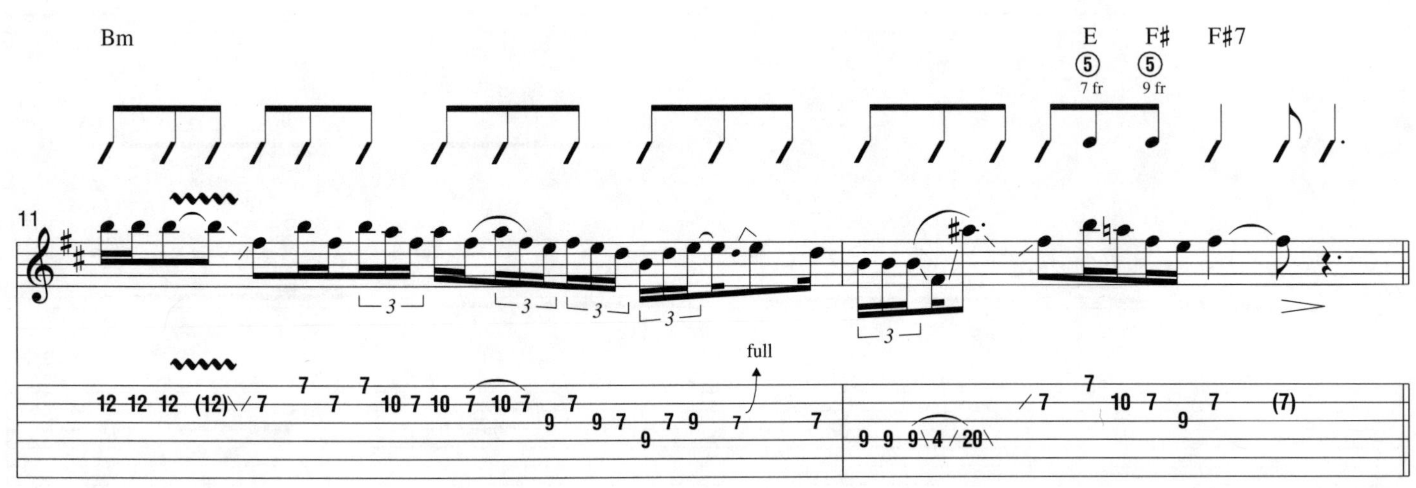
Bm
E
F♯
F♯7
full

Figure 8 - Outro Guitar Solo

In measures 10 (iv) and 11 (i) of the first chorus of the outro solo, Buddy tears into a series of bends, releases, and pull-offs (see measure 10 of Fig. 7) at warp speed. Notice how the same notes (F♯, E, and D) function as the 9th, root, and ♭7th (implying an extended minor 9th tonality) over the iv chord, and as the 5th, 4th, and ♭3rd (implying a groovy minor add4 tonality) over the i chord. In addition, the hypnotic repetition, combined with the swooping nature of the lick, drives this number home like a punch in the ear.

16

17

Featured Guitar:
Gtr. 1 meas. 10-11

Slow Demo:
Gtr. 1 meas. 10-11

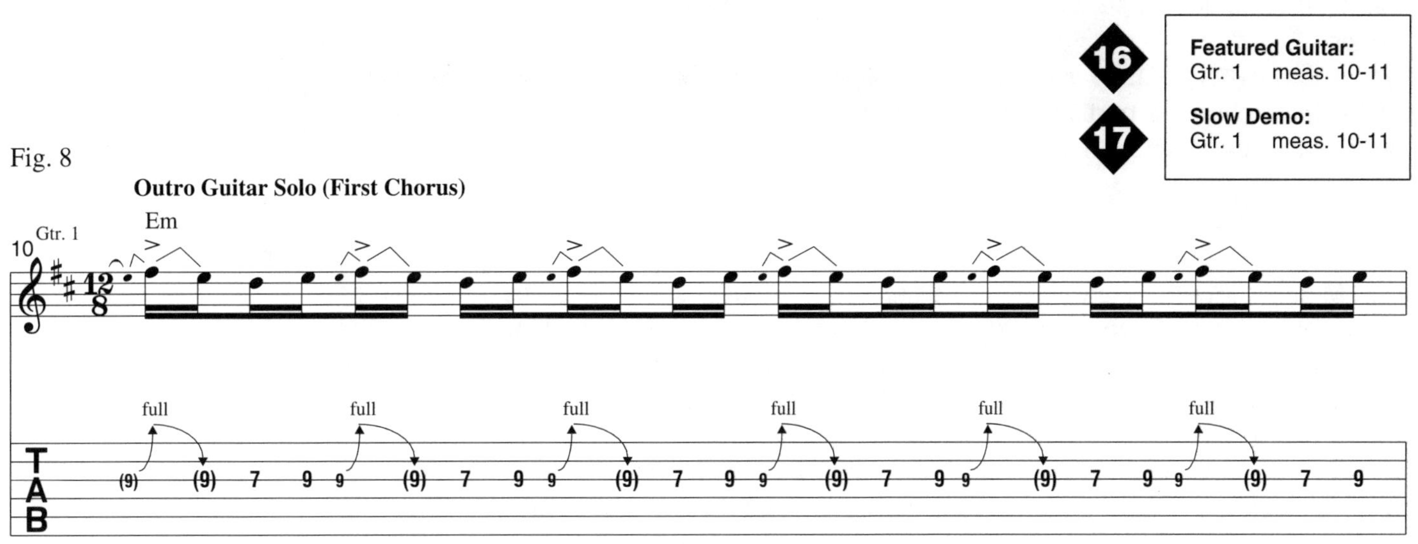

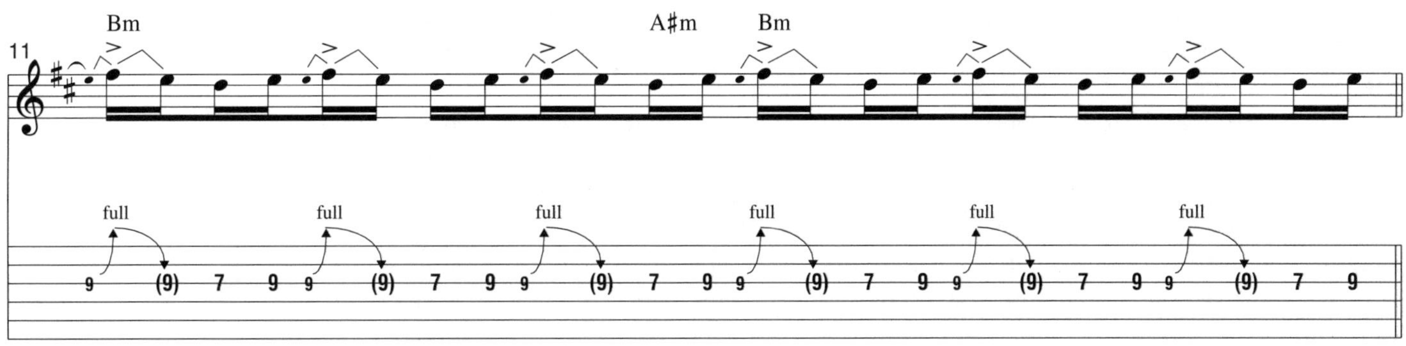

SHE'S OUT THERE SOMEWHERE
(Stone Crazy)

By Buddy Guy

From the same epochal LP as "I Smell a Rat," "She's Out There Somewhere" is a positively joyous shuffle blues. The groove is relaxed and effortless, with the rhythm instruments playing in muted tones to allow Buddy's crackling Strat to ride comfortably on top.

The head of the tune is based upon sound blues principles regarding the indication of the chord changes, particularly the I and IV chords. These forms are quite versatile and could easily be adapted to other songs.

Figure 9 - Intro

Measures 1–4 (I chord) utilize triads along with double and triple stops that reinforce the tonality of the I (F) chord. Buddy executes the one-measure phrase that serves as the increment by sliding into F/C (root and 5th) with his index finger, followed by D/B♭ (6th and 4th) played with his ring finger. (Note: This latter double stop could imply a fast change to the IV chord, which would then resolve back to the implied I chord with the first inversion F triad, accessed via a hammer-on with the middle finger from the ♭3rd (A♭) to the major 3rd (A). A pickup note of the major 3rd occurs on beat 4 in measures 1 and 2. The ♭3rd that occurs as a pickup in measure 3 is probably a mistake. However, in measure 4 it leads into the IV (B♭) chord change in measure 5.

Measures 5 and 6 (IV chord) present a similar sequence with the significant difference of the A♭ note taking the place of the A note. This concept cannot be overemphasized. The modulation of the major 3rd to the ♭3rd (in relationship to the I chord) is the strongest and hippest way to indicate a change from the I chord to the IV chord, due to the ♭3rd functioning as the ♭7th tone over the IV chord.

Measures 7 and 8 (I chord) repeat the basic increment in a similar fashion as measures 1–4. In measure 9 (V chord) Buddy opts to spring into the root position of the F basic blues scale at the octave (fret 13). Notice that he bends to the root (C) on beat 1 and then repeats the C note in conjunction with the ♭7th (B♭), thereby accentuating the C dominant tonality. For measure 10 (IV chord), he bends and vibratos to the F (5th) before slipping in the double-stop pattern for the IV chord from measures 5 and 6. The insertion of single-note lines adds dynamics by contrasting the double-stop patterns throughout the intro. By starting back in on the main pattern of the intro on beat 3, Buddy eases the transition to the I chord in measure 11. Be aware of the major 3rd (A) making its appearance again in the lick for the I (F) chord in measures 11 and 12.

As you listen to the entire tune, notice how Buddy continually works in variations on the intro patterns, including a metamorphosis into Elmore James's "Dust My Broom" lick!

18
19
Featured Guitar:
Gtr. 1 meas. 1-12
Slow Demo:
Gtr. 1 meas. 1-12
F5 F6 B♭5 B♭6 C5 C6
Fig. 9
Intro
Moderate Blues ♩. = 111
Gtr. 2 (clean)
Gtr. 1 (dist.)
mf
*f
sim.
1/4
full
(cont. in notation)
N.C.(F)
* Control dynamics w/ vol. knob throughout.

YOU'VE BEEN GONE TOO LONG
(Stone Crazy)

By Buddy Guy

Nowhere is the "Hendrix connection" clearer than on this modal blues-rocker. Echoes of "Voodoo Chile" and "Hear My Train a Comin'" abound. Unfortunately, this is a too-rare example of this style for Buddy, as he has a real affinity for stretching out over a cool one-chord romp.

Figure 10 - Intro

The two-measure phrase around which this song is built functions as the head, the hook, and the rhythm pattern. Based upon the E basic blues scale (or minor pentatonic, if you prefer), it uses the 5th (B), ♭7th (D), root (E), and ♭3rd (G) notes, with the root appearing in two octaves at three different fret positions. Slide into the B at fret 7 with your ring finger, using a logical combination of your index and ring fingers for the rest of the notes in this box. Hammer from the A (grace note) to B with your index and ring fingers, also, in measure 2. After picking the low, open E string, execute the quarter-step bend on the G note with your middle finger, followed by your index for the octave E note on string 4 at fret 2. End with the open E string and repeat (as necessary!).

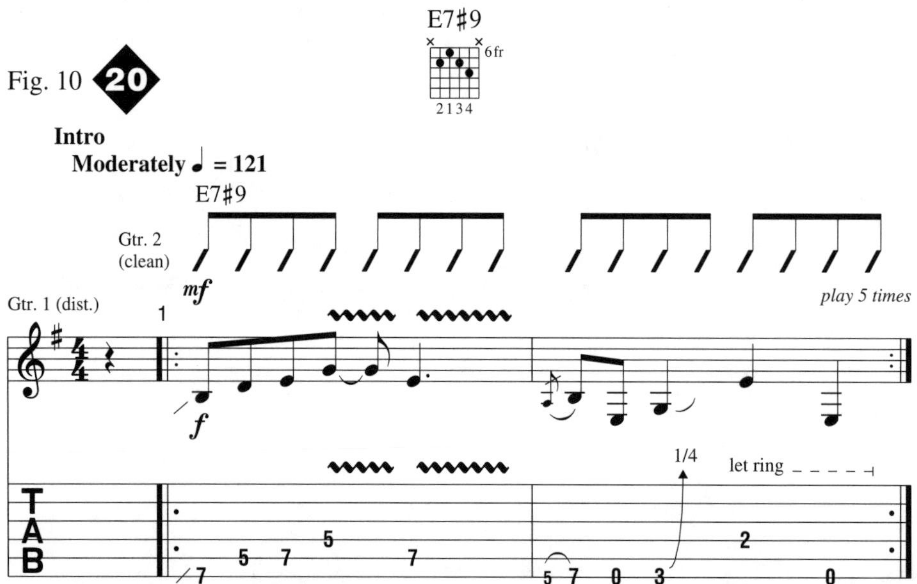

Figure 11 - Riff

The rhythm pattern played by brother Phil (Gtr. 2) is a clever variation on the opening theme that Buddy played. Rhythmically different, it contains the same notes, with the addition of the G/D (♭3rd and ♭7th) double stop on beat 2 of measure 1. Where Phil had strummed a hip E7♯9 chord in Fig. 10, he now substitutes this riff for the underpinning, playing it in a similar way for the entire tune. Harmonically, an Em7 tonality is implied.

Figure 12 - Guitar Solo

Practically every measure of this tour-de-force is worthy of our scrutiny, but measures 9–18 of the second guitar solo, in particular, show Buddy's brilliance. Kicking the groove into overdrive, he regales us with a syncopated double-stop pattern consisting of the E (root) note at fret 5 on string 2 combined with the open, high E string. Intuitively (and correctly!) holding the tension with this lick for four measures, he starts to release his hold on our imaginations by flipping a few notes, all on string 1, in the second position box of the E minor pentatonic scale. Dig that in this type of tune (no chord changes), the pitches of the notes in this measure are not as important as the rhythmic feel.

In measure 14, Buddy surprises us with a descending series of inverted triads (E/B, E♭/B♭, and D/A) that lend weight, texture, and harmony. In measure 15, he begins to tip his hand (figuratively speaking, of course) by hopping down to the open, root position of the E blues scale. Emphasis is placed on the G note (♭3rd, for that minor-key flavor) with descending notes leading to hammers and pulls involving the open strings and the fretted root notes. On beats 3 and 4 of measure 16, with the open low E and the quarter-step bend of G, we see that Buddy's plan was to arrive back at a pattern (measures 17 and 18) similar to the hook of the tune.

What has been demonstrated on "You've Been Gone Too Long" is a superb sense of composition. This is a skill not easily acquired, or even explained, for that matter. Much practice is required, involving trial and error, in order to assess when to repeat an idea or move on to a new one. Naturally, listening to masters of the form like Buddy Guy and Jimi Hendrix will help you develop your own approach.

22
Featured Guitar:
Gtr. 2 meas. 9-19
23
Slow Demo:
Gtr. 2 meas. 9-19
Fig. 12
Guitar Solo

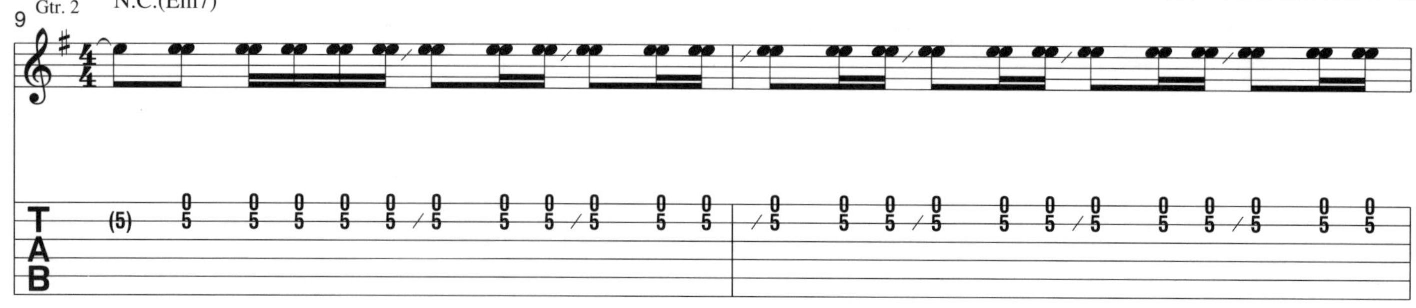
Gtr. 2
N.C.(Em7)

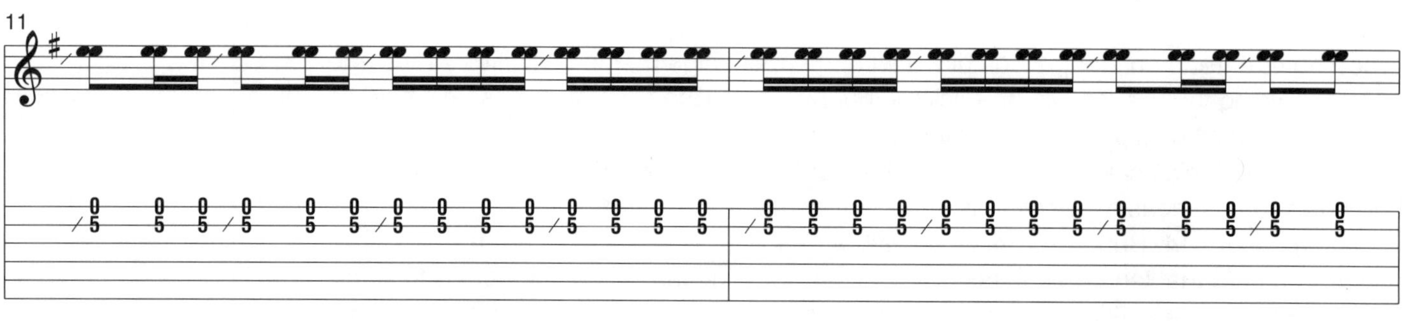

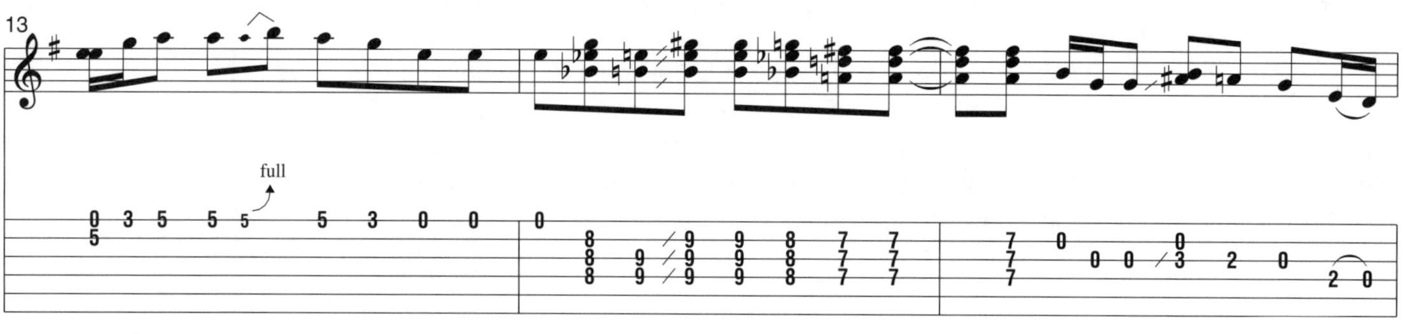
full

let ring
1/4
let ring
let ring

BUDDY'S BLUES (BUDDY'S BOOGIE)

(The Dollar Done Fell)

Written by Buddy Guy

Saving him from the completely unjust lack of interest shown by American record companies, the English JSP label kept Buddy's music in front of his public during the eighties. Ironically, this album was recorded live at Buddy's Checkerboard Lounge in Chicago. At any rate, though the sound quality is somewhat primitive, the performances are spontaneous and inspired.

"Buddy's Blues" contains the classic octave-bass pattern that he helped to popularize in the sixties. An instrumental showcase for Buddy, it once again spotlights the organic flow of ideas when his fingers take flight.

Figure 13 - Intro

The bass pattern for the I (G), IV (C), and V (D) chords is basically the same, relative to the changes. Hence, seeing the pattern for the I chord gives you the idea for the other two changes. Note, however, that Buddy alternates two different patterns for the I chord. The first, in measures 1 and 3, is a straightforward reading of the traditional sequence of the root (G), octave, ♭7th (F), and 5th (D). Measure 2 (and by inference, measure 4, but we will get to that) contains a rhythmic variation, as the octave and ♭7th notes are phrased as triplets on beat 3, as are the ♭7th and 5th notes on beat 4.

Now, about measure 4: being way too creative to merely recycle the basic pattern, Buddy plays two quarter-note triplets with the root (G), 3rd (B), 5th (D), ♭7th (F), root, and ♭3rd (B♭) bent a bluesy quarter step. No such embellishments occur on the other chord changes.

* Control dynamics w/ vol. knob throughout.
** Chord symbols reflect overall tonality.

Figure 14 - Guitar Solo (Second Chorus)

Though unquestionably known as a lead guitarist, Buddy (like one of his idols, B.B. King) can play rhythm. Measures 1–4 of the second chorus of the solo have tasty triple-stop dominant forms based on the I7 chord. In measure 1, he plays, with his index finger, what functions as the top three notes of a G9 chord: F (♭7th), A (9th), and D (5th). That same voicing, moved up to fret 11 on beat 4, operates as an *appoggiatura* (a discordant note or chord falling on the beat). In measure 2, he gets downright funky with the 3rd (B), ♭7th (F), and ♯9th (A♯) notes implying a G7♯9 chord. (Low to high, use your index, middle, and ring fingers.) Hold on to your hats for measure 3: Buddy moves the 7♯9 form up the neck chromatically from fret 9 to frets 10 and 11. Theoretically speaking, this would imply Gmaj7sus4 (!) at fret 10 and G11♭5 (!) at fret 11. Yikes! In blues terms, we would have to look at this as a dominant form being moved organically up and back (see measure 4) for tension and release.

Figure 15 - Guitar Solo 2 (Fifth chorus)

The fifth chorus of solo 2 highlights Buddy's remarkable ability to riff with taste and control in the upper reaches of the fretboard. Let us suss it out measure by measure.

Measure 1 (I7): Buddy connects a lazy 1½-step bend at fret 19 on the B string (F♯ to A, the major 7th and 9th) to a two-step bend (up to A♯, the ♯9th) with his ring finger. The average blues guitarist might have opened with the root, but Buddy loves to step way out on the branch, rarely falling off.

Measure 2 (I7): Doing the unexpected, Buddy starts a new bend from the F♯, this time just going up a half step to the root and vibratoing for three beats of sweet release. Be sure to back up your ring finger with your middle and index.

Measure 3 (I7): Building his composition with themes and repetition, Buddy repeats the bend from measure 1.

Measure 4 (I7): Continuing with his "call and response" routine, Buddy repeats the half-step bend from measure 2, coming off it with the F♯ (major 7th) and D (5th) notes at fret 19 (both notes played with the ring finger) before…

Measure 5 (IV7): ...bending up the G string at fret 19 (D, the 9th) to E (3rd) two times with the ring finger. After the second bend, Buddy releases the bend back to D and drops down to fret 17 for the vibratoed root (C) note with his index finger. Coming into the first measure of a new chord change with the major 3rd and/or the ♭7th is the best way to establish tonality.

Measure 6 (IV7): Buddy maintains the C dominant tonality by picking the ♭7th (B♭) with the 5th (G). He then plays a favorite lick of his and many other "modern" electric blues guitarists. Bending the root (C) a full step at fret 17 on the G string with his ring finger, Buddy holds the pitch at D (9th) while simultaneously picking the F (4th) at fret 18 on the B string with his pinky. The resulting blend (a hip dominant tonality if you think of the 4th as an 11th) tickles the ear while Buddy re-bends the G string. This thrilling "outside" harmony begs to resolve to the...

Measure 7 (I7): ...root (G), but no! Buddy has other ideas and decides to keep the pot boiling by sustaining and vibratoing the D (5th) with his ring finger for two long beats. He then restrikes the C and reaches back two frets with his index finger and pushes the B♭ (♭3rd) back up to the C, with vibrato! Even with light-gauge strings, this maneuver takes considerable strength. It is helpful to grip the edge of the neck tightly with the thumb and squeeze with your whole hand as you work the G string with your index finger.

Measure 8 (I7): Anchoring his hand in the root position box of the G blues scale at fret 15, Buddy finally achieves a resolution as he combines the root (G) with the ♭3rd (B♭), major 3rd (B—very nice), and ♭7th (F). G dominant tonality at last! Staying in the box, Buddy hits an unusual, low octave B on string 5 (fret 14) with his middle finger before picking the ♭7th with his index finger (on string 4) and...

Measure 9 (V7): ...sliding it up to the G (4th) over the V (D) chord. After a brief, teasing vibrato, Buddy runs down the blues scale in the root position, nicking the root (D) before sustaining the gritty ♭3rd (F). Though he has given us some sweet major 3rds and 5ths during this blues chorus, he seems intent on making a musical statement based on the more unstable notes, such as the 4th, from the blues scale.

Measure 10 (IV7): Having found a home at the root position G blues scale at fret 15, Buddy skips up to string 2 and bends the 4th (F) again (!) a full step to the 5th (G) with his pinky. Shifting fingers quickly, he bends the root (C) up a full step to the 9th (D). He then picks the root again and throws in the D/B♭ (9th and ♭7th) dyad as subtle tension (and a preview of the turnaround measures) to resolve to...

Measure 11 (I7): ...the root (G) via the ♭3rd (B♭). Not willing to get too comfortable, however, he plays a combination of bluesy double stops (D/B♭ and E/C), bending the latter two strings up a full and half step, releasing, and re-bending into the next measure. This is really all about abstract sound at this point, rather than specific pitches against specific chords. The effect draws our attention to the end of this chorus in preparation for the next one (not shown), which takes a different direction.

Make the double-stop, double-string bends with your ring and pinky (low to high) or with your ring finger by pulling down towards the floor. (This is the way that Chuck Berry accesses this bend.) Once again, you need strong fingers and a good grip on the edge of the neck with your thumb.

Measure 12 (I7): Maintaining the double-string bend across the bar line, Buddy resolves very briefly to the root (G) before slapping the E/C and D/B♭ double stops, ending this segment of his solo with a sneer.

26 **Featured Guitar:** Gtr. 3 meas. 1-12

27 **Slow Demo:** Gtr. 3 meas. 1-12

DEDICATION TO THE LATE T-BONE WALKER

(D.J. Play My Blues)

Written by Buddy Guy

To this day, Buddy will often pay tribute to his influences during live performances—making a point of playing a little John Lee Hooker, Jimmy Reed, or Muddy Waters to make sure his audience never forgets where the music started. In the seventies and eighties, two of the regulars he would imitate to a "T" were T-Bone Walker and Freddie King. In 1981, he waxed one of these tributes on the best album he recorded between *Stone Crazy* and *Damn Right, I've Got the Blues.*

Buddy's rampaging guitar playing would seem to owe little to the jazzy and urbane stylings of the "father of electric blues," but underneath all that fire and brimstone are the tasty runs and bends of Aaron Walker. T-Bone spent forty years in the root position blues box, milking it for all it was worth. Buddy, along with every other blues guitar great, has also mastered this deceptively simple scale.

Figure 16 - Intro and Guitar Solo

The two-measure intro and first 12-bar blues chorus contain a wealth of T-Bone-isms.

Measure 1 of intro (I7): One of "'Bone's" classic intros. Forming a standard 9th chord voicing on string 5 with his middle, index, and ring (as a barre) fingers, Buddy moves this chord shape down by half steps from the twelfth fret to the ninth fret, strumming each chord in the sequence. Combining the 5th on string 1 and (sometimes) the 9th on string 2 from the barre under his ring finger, he also adds in the 13th on string 1 with his pinky. This is done on the I (A9), VII (A♭9), ♭VII (G9), and VI (F♯9) chords. Do not let this unaccompanied 15/8 measure throw you. The time is very free in this section: Buddy is interested in bringing in the feeling of a T-Bone intro as well as the actual notes. You should also know that another, more typical way that Walker would play an intro like this would be with the I9, ♭VII9, ♭VI9, and V9 chords, ending on the V+.

Measure 2 of intro (I7): Buddy arpeggiates the V+ chord. Finger this spicy little chord (that cries out to resolve to the I chord) with your ring, middle, and index (as a barre on strings 3 and 2 at fret 5) fingers. The B♭9 (sans root) chord on beat 4, functioning as a passing chord to the I9 in measure 1 of the blues chorus, is another favorite T-Bone voicing that slides well, sounding like a horn section modulating between chords. Play it with your index, ring, middle, and pinky fingers, low to high.

Measure 1 (I9): Resolving to the I9 chord and using it as a springboard into his improvisation, Buddy bends the 4th (D) up a full step to the 5th (E), descending to the ♭3rd (C) and then backing up to the 4th before resolving to the root (A). B.B. King also plays similar patterns, being profoundly influenced by T-Bone himself. The fingering that he seems to use involves crossing the middle finger over the ring when going from the 4th to the root.

Measure 2 (IV9): Buddy peals off a long, eighth- and sixteenth-note phrase that runs for two measures. In this measure of the IV chord, the A, C, D, and bent E notes function as the 5th, ♭7th, root, and 9th, nailing the D dominant tonality.

Measure 3 (I9): Even at this leisurely pace (♩. = 50), there are a lot of notes in this measure. Restricting himself to the root (A), ♭3rd (C), 4th (D), ♭7th (G), and 5th (E), Buddy zips through a string (pun intended) of sixteenth notes in triplet form. The serpentine quality and tight focus of this measure adds tension (despite the note selection) that is only released in the next measure of the I chord by the use of musical space—certainly not by the last note, D (4th), that Buddy ends with.

Measure 4 (I9): The amount of space left in the beginning of this measure is breathtaking after all that note manipulation. When Buddy does pick up the gauntlet again, he jumps to the two top strings to dynamically contrast the bass notes of the preceding measure. The triplet phrase is a common one, including the ♭3rd (C), root (A), and 5th (E) notes, but it does help to restart the momentum again.

Measure 5 (IV9): Buddy stays on the top two strings to facilitate the transition to the IV chord. Using all of the notes from the A basic blues scale in this measure, but with emphasis on the two middle strings, he then accentuates the IV-chord tonality with the root (D), ♭7th (C), and 5th (A). Be sure to catch the subtlety of the root being bent one half step to the ♭9 (E♭) on beats 2 and 3. It adds a bit of tension that is released by the root notes that follow.

Measure 6 (IV9): Dynamically shifting back to the top two strings again, Buddy converts the C, A, and E notes used in measure 4 of the I chord into the ♭7th, 5th, and cool 9th notes. On beat 3, he moves to the two middle strings with the ♭7th, root, and 5th notes, which become the…

Measure 7 (I9): …♭3rd (C), 4th (D), and root (A) notes in measure 7. With a sustained and vibratoed root as resolution, Buddy intensifies the moment as he inserts a triple-stop A7 form on beat 2. He then plays a classic T-Bone run down the scale (including the requisite bend of the 4th to the 5th on string 3) that ends on the tangy ♭3rd (C), but resolves comfortably on the…

Measure 8 (I9): …root (A). On beat 2, Buddy slips briefly into the A Mixolydian mode by picking the 6th (F♯) and bending it one half step to the ♭7th (G) and releasing it. It is a subtle moment, but adds to the overall color of the measure. Staying with the sweet melodic concept a bit longer, he includes the major 3rd (C♯) in his next phrase on beats 3 and 4.

Measure 9 (V9): Sliding up to the root (E) on string 3 with his ring finger, followed by the root on string 2 with his index finger, Buddy performs another classic T-Bone move. Chuck Berry appropriated this lick early in his career, but he bent the 4th to the 5th on string 3 (over the I chord, in this instance) for a more aggressive feel.

Measure 10 (IV9): Starting his next phrase with E (9th), G (4th), and A (5th), Buddy repeatedly bends the ♭7th (C) a quarter step to one of the true "blue notes" in between the ♭7th and the major 7th. The delicious musical tension of this bend sets the stage for the coming resolution to the I chord in measure 11 and is the type of quarter-step bend that separates the real blues guitarist from the mere dilettante (Hint: it's worth the time to master).

On beat 4 Buddy begins running down the scale, again ending the measure on the C (♭7th) note on string 3 at fret 5 as a way of working down to the…

Measure 11 (I9 and IV9): …root (A) on beat 1 of the turnaround. Beat 2 has another classic T-Bone lick involving the 4th (D) bent to the 5th (E), followed by the fretted 5th, root, and 6th (F♯) bent one half step to the ♭7th (G). Beats 3 and 4 (IV9) utilize the E, F♯, D, C, and A notes functioning as the 9th, major 3rd, root, ♭7th, and 5th notes of D. Through the careful manipulation of the same set of notes, Buddy indicates the I-to-IV chord change with panache.

Measure 12 (I9 and V9): After resolving to the I chord with the ♭3rd (C) and root (A) notes, Buddy skewers beat 2 with a lick including the E (5th), D (4th), C (♭3th), A (root), and G (♭7th), before ending on the ♭7th (D) of the V chord on beat 3.

A9
D9
B♭9
E♭9
A9 XI
B♭9 XII
E9
28
29
Featured Guitars:
Gtr. 1 meas. 1-14
Slow Demos:
Gtr. 1 meas. 1-2
Gtr. 1 meas. 3-14
Fig. 16
Intro
Free Time
Gtr. 1 (clean)
A♭9
G9
F♯9
N.C.(E+)
mf
let ring
Guitar Solo
Slow Blues ♩. = 50
* Gtr. 2 (clean)
mp
full
* Two gtrs. arr. for one.
1/2

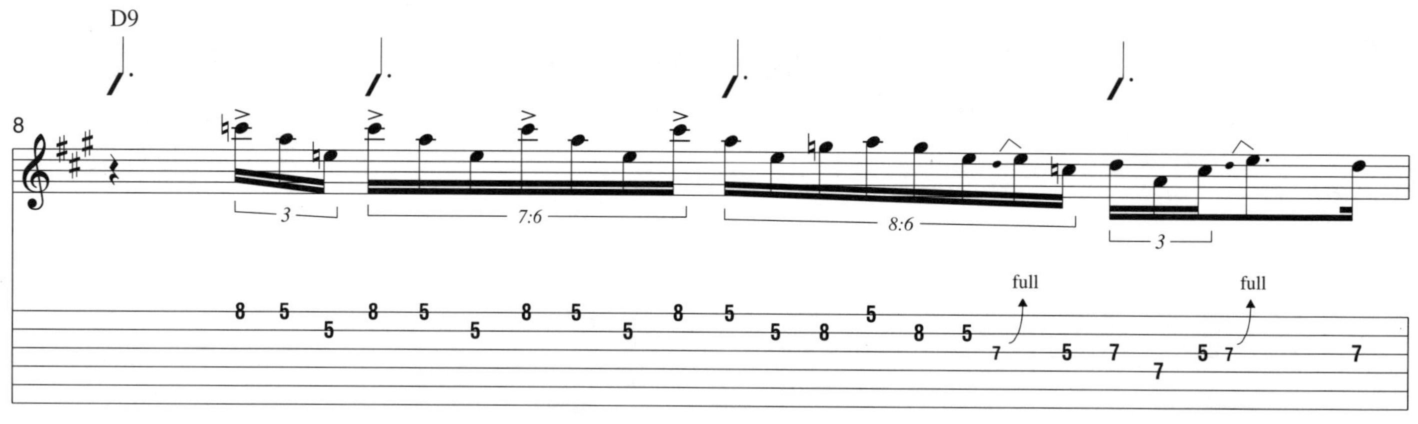
D9
full
full

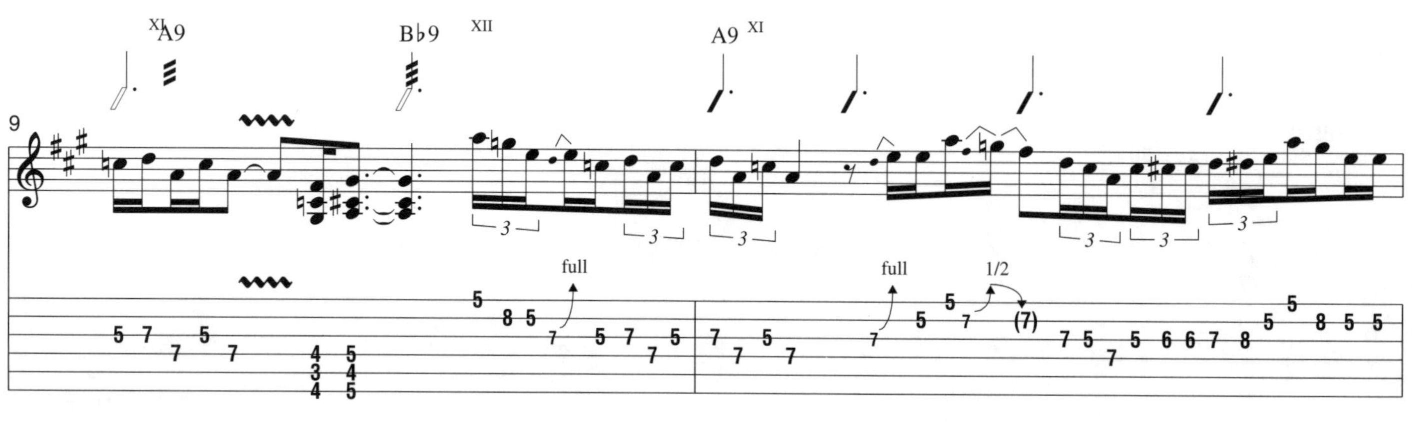
A9
B♭9
A9
full
full
1/2

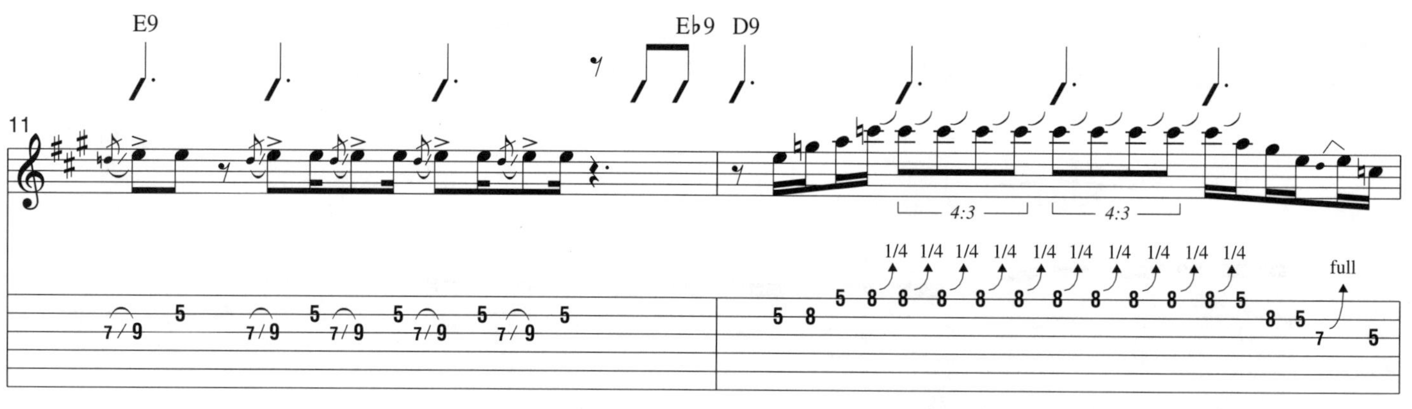
E9
E♭9
D9
full

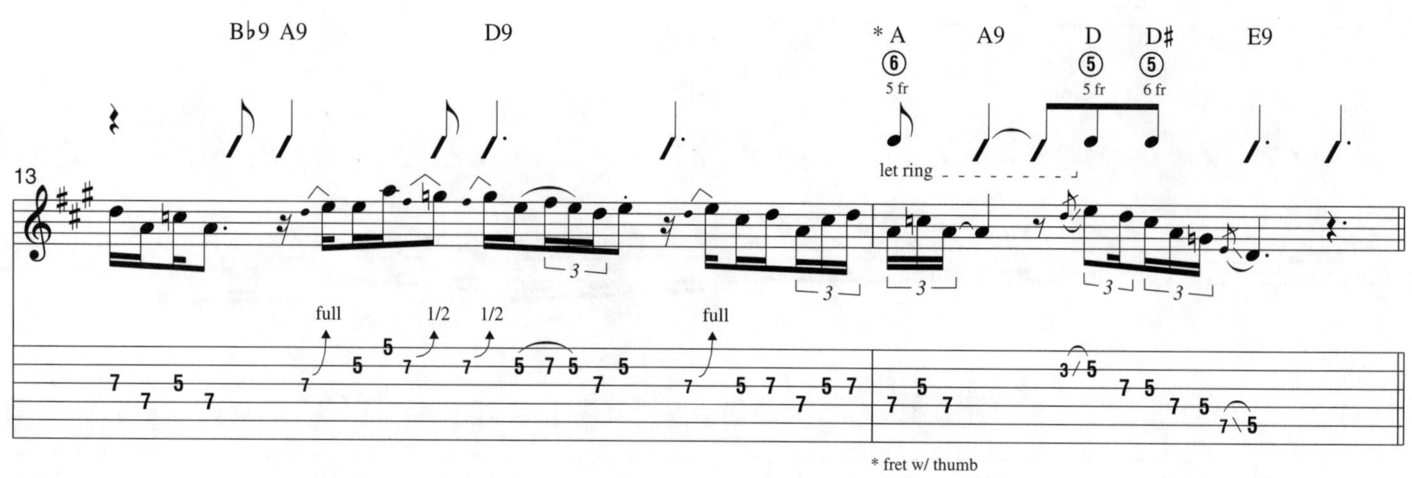
B♭9
A9
D9
* A
A9
D
D♯
E9
5 fr
5 fr
6 fr
let ring
full
1/2
1/2
full

* fret w/ thumb

BLUES AT MY BABY'S HOUSE

(D.J. Play My Blues)

Written by Buddy Guy

Somewhat similar to "I Small a Rat," this long, minor key meditation has passages of great intensity dynamically contrasted with shifts in volume and phrasing. The second chorus of the first guitar solo shows Buddy at his "over-the-top" best, while also demonstrating his skill at composing within a solo by using a theme and repetition.

Figure 17 - Guitar Solo (Second chorus)

Measure 1 (i7): Flailing like a banshee, Buddy rips through the G/E (♭7th and 5th) dyad with furious tremolo picking. Use your ring and middle fingers for the dyad so your hand will be in the most advantageous position to make the bends in the octave, root position box of the A minor pentatonic scale that follow. Throughout this entire blues chorus, Buddy is working to achieve an effect or feeling from the notes he attacks, rather than making a melodic/harmonic statement. That said, he still has the presence of mind (or instinct from doing this for so long) to create even *more* tension with the bends that resolve down to the…

Measure 2 (i7): ♭3rd (C, the target note in A minor). Working the fingerboard like a piece of soft clay, Buddy drops down to the root position at fret 5 for a set of blistering thirty-second and sixteenth notes based around the ♭3rd, root, 4th (D), and 4th bent to the ♭5th (E♭) and 5th (E). Resolving once again to the root, Buddy shifts positions to box 2 at fret 8 with the root, ♭3rd, and 4th notes, ending on the ♭3rd (implying minor tonality) before taking a dramatic rest of a little more than a full beat.

Measure 3 (i7): As he is known to do, Buddy repeats the tremolo picking from measure 1, followed by rapid-fire scale notes. In this way, he establishes a two-measure theme that only heightens our anticipation for what will come next.

Measure 4 (i7): Zooming up to fret 20 (the octave position 2 of the A minor pentatonic scale) with his index finger, Buddy hammers the G (♭7th) to the A (root) and vibratoes before launching into a wild series of notes on string 3. The 5th, ♭5th, and 4th notes cry out for resolution to the root, which Buddy briefly provides near the end of beat 3. Not yet ready to surrender, however, he quickly follows with a nasty double stop (C/G) that gives the minor 7th tonality one last shot before he shoots down to the…

Measure 5 (iv7): …second position box at fret 8 with the D (root), C (♭7th), and A (5th) notes to announce the change to the IVm chord. Sliding down further yet, Buddy lands in the root position at fret 5, where he wrings out the root, ♭7th, and 5th notes before bending the root to the cool 9th (E) and vibratoing for maximum effect. He then repeats, almost as a motif, the ♭7th, 5th, and root notes, tacking on a subtle quarter-step bend from the ♭7th (for tension at the end of the phrase, of course) and rests again.

Measure 6 (iv7): …Back up to position 2, Buddy kicks around the root, 9th, ♭7th, 5th, and ♭9th notes. Dig how the 9th and ♭9th notes extend the minor tonality past the minor seventh. As he did in measure 5, Buddy shifts near the middle of the measure down to the root position once again, using the same notes (an octave lower for contrast) to correspond to the tonality of the iv7 chord change. Looking at the bends mixed in with sixteenth and thirty-second notes, you should realize that one must have a confident sense of how far to push the strings to approach the proper pitch. Practice, naturally, and also a certain lack of inhibition helps!

Measure 7 (i7): After bending the ♭3rd (C) up a full step to the 4th (D) with his *index* finger and releasing back to C to reestablish the minor tonality, Buddy hops down to strings 4 and 5 to add contrast to all that upper-register riffing that went on previously.

Once there, he invents a little riff with the 4th (D), 5th (E), ♭7th (G), and root (A) notes that he repeats before moving down to strings 5 and 6 with the 4th, ♭3rd (C), and root notes. Continuing to descend down through the scale, he plays the…

Measure 8 (i7): …root and open E string. Feeling the need to jack things back up again in preparation for the impending V chord in measure 10, Buddy zips up to the root and second positions on strings 1 and 2. While there, he picks on the 5th (E), root (A), ♭7th (G), ♭3rd (C), and 4th (D) notes from the A minor pentatonic scale.

Measure 9 (v7): With his index and ring fingers, Buddy hammers the root (E) to the 9th (F♯), followed by the hip ♭9th (F) and root notes on string 1. From here on through the rest of the measure, Buddy adjusts his fingering (and his thinking) to laying in the root position of the E minor pentatonic scale between frets 12 and 15. This literal change of scale to match the chord change is not something Buddy does often; however, it is very effective here and in measure 10. The F♯ notes in this measure could be considered to have come from the E Aeolian mode, with the F functioning as an appoggiatura. The tenth fret A note at the end of beat 4 shows that Buddy has repositioned his hand so he is ready for the…

Measure 10 (iv7): …D minor pentatonic scale between frets 10 and 13. Buddy lingers here for two beats, vibratoing sweetly on the bent 5th (A) before heading back down to the root position of the Aminor pentatonic scale at fret 5 on beats 3 and 4. There he leans heavily on the root, 9th, and ♭7th notes. (Note: The E note on beat 1 could be considered as belonging to the D Aeolian mode, while the E♭ is a passing note.)

Measure 11 (i7): Banging down three times on the root in no uncertain terms to establish the tonic chord change, Buddy proceeds to accentuate the root with a bend and vibrato while embellishing all around it with the 5th (E), ♭7th (G), 4th (D), and ♭3rd (C) notes.

Measure 12 (i7 and v7): Continuing his run from measure 11, Buddy goes through the ♭3rd (C), 4th (D), and root notes before resolving the measure (and this solo) on the root (E) of the v7 chord with his index finger.

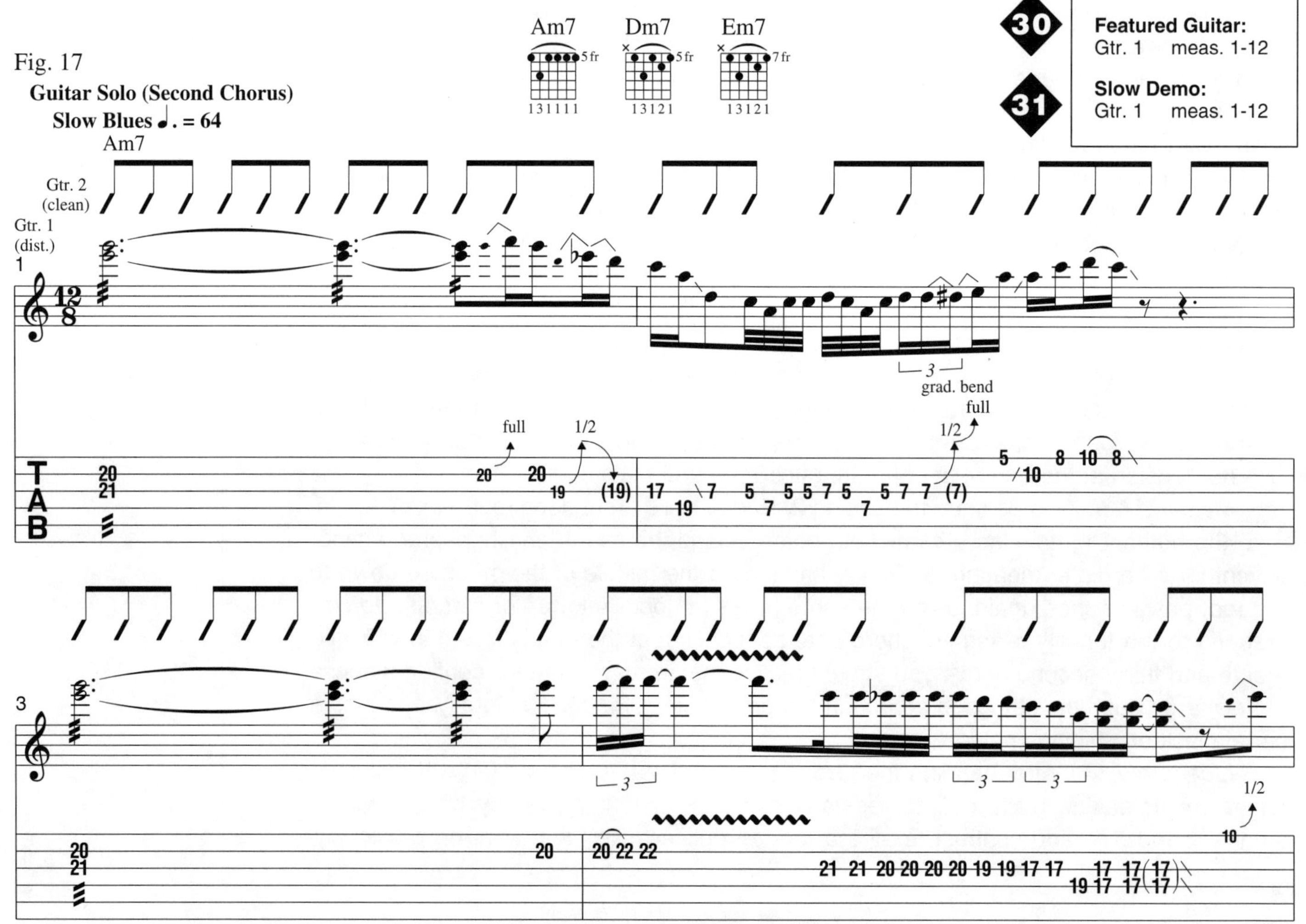

Dm7
full
1/4
1/2
Am7
Em7
Gtr. 2: w/ Rhy. Fill
Rhy. Fill
Gtr. 2
let ring

SHE SUITS ME TO A TEE
(D.J. Play My Blues)

Words and Music by Buddy Guy

Buddy's tribute to Elmore James has a similar groove (and vibe) to "She Is Out There." In addition, it also recalls B.B. King's non-slide tribute to Elmore, "Please Love Me" (1953).

Figure 18 - Intro

Buddy imitates Elmore's "Dust My Broom" slide lick in measure 1 by barring with his index finger on strings 1 and 2 at fret 12. All downstrokes, plus an aggressive attitude, is helpful in conveying the proper feel. In measure 2, he pulls down on the ♭3rd (G) with his index finger, raising it a quarter step to the "blue note" in between the ♭3rd and the major 3rd (G♯). He then resolves to the root (E) on string 4 with his ring finger.

Like his idol B.B. King, Buddy has not played slide guitar on record.

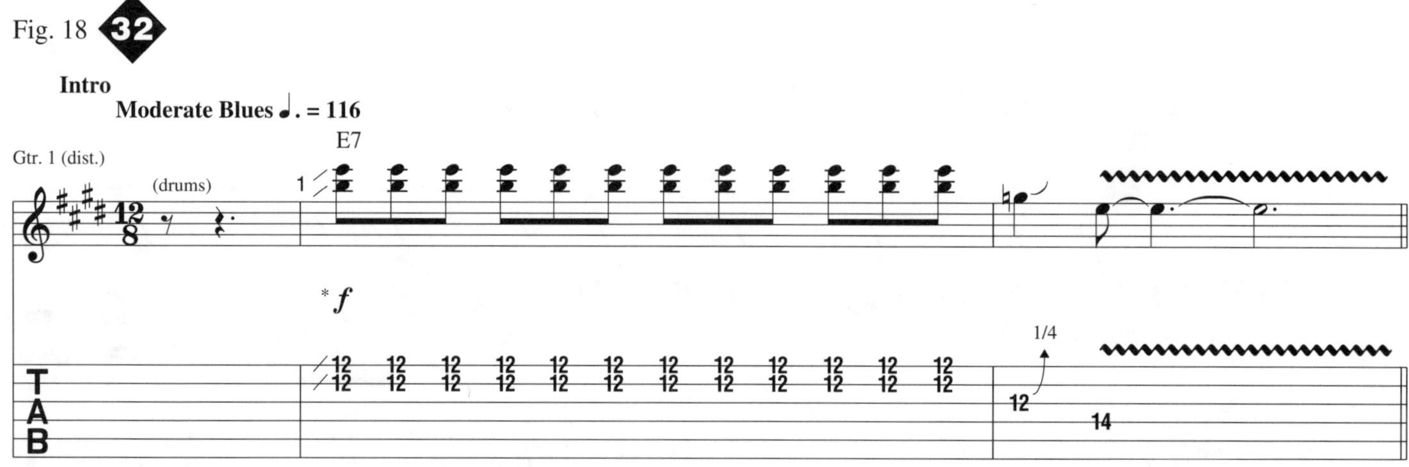

Figure 19 - Verse Lick

In measure 7 of verse 2, Buddy plays a neat little lick with his pick and middle finger over the I7 (E7) chord. Barring with his index finger at fret 2 (F♯/A), he picks string 3 with his pick and string 1 with his middle finger. He then slides up to fret 3 (G/B♭) and pulls off from the A (4th) with his index finger to the open G (♭3rd), resolving to the root (E) on string 4. Notice how the G/B♭ makes for a mighty tasty blues tonality.

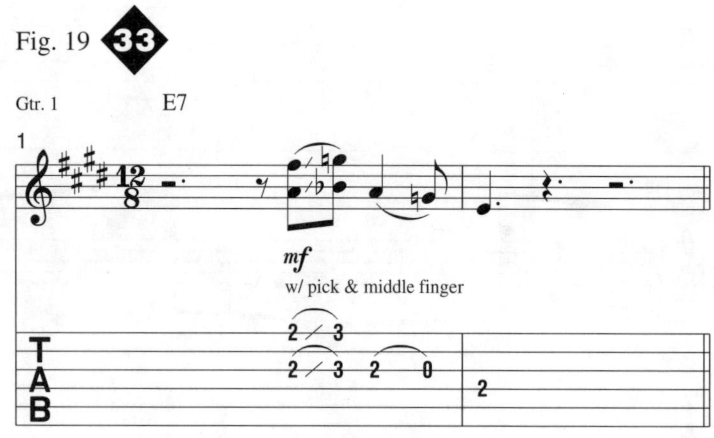

Figure 20 - Ending Tag

The four-measure, free time "tag" at the end of the tune has Buddy playing "backwards" on each string (in measure 2) down through the E basic blues scale. This is not something you would want to do too often, but it provides a surprise at the conclusion of "She Suits Me to a Tee." Buddy is most likely using his index and ring fingers to play each pair of notes.

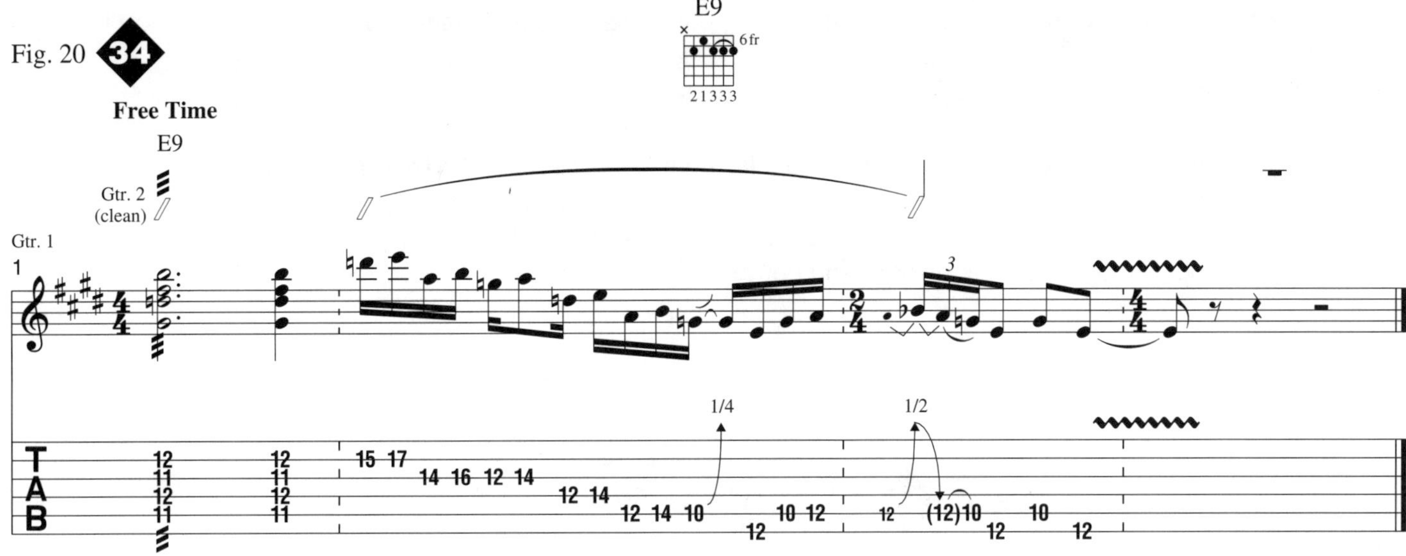

JUST TEASIN'
(D.J. Play My Blues)

Written by Buddy Guy

Eric Clapton has mentioned in interviews that he wished he'd been able to tape many more of his inspired performances. Buddy Guy may very well feel the same way; however, "Just Teasin'" surely represents him at his unpredictable best. This medium shuffle instrumental is chock full of progressive blues tonalities and time-warp phrasing. It sounds extremely spontaneous, as if Buddy counted it off, got right into the "zone," and ran with it. This piece is a prime example of creative freedom—one that we should all aspire to.

Figure 21 - Intro

Buddy announces his intention to go for the jugular right from measure 1. Using his ring and pinky fingers, he plays the tart C♭/F (♭3rd and 6th) double stop, followed by the root (A♭) and 6th. To start off at this high a level of intensity would spell disaster for most other guitarists, but Buddy only goes onward and upward from here.

Figure 22 - "Outside" Lick

In measures 10 (IV chord) and 11 (I chord) of the first chorus, Buddy goes "outside" with his note selection. In measure 10, after sliding in with the F♯ (4th), he follows with the A (♯5th) and A♭ (5th) notes. He ends the measure on B♭ (6th) bent a half step, with his ring finger, to B (♭7th) across the bar line (where it becomes a spicy ♭3rd), and then a whole step to the major 3rd (C) target note. Buddy frequently returns to the C throughout as a harmonious diatonic note to balance all the dissonance he throws at us.

His resolution to the root in measure 11 is brief as he ends on the F (6th) and C. Be aware that although Buddy careens above and around the blues scale in this piece, he regularly checks in with chord tones and target notes that identify the chord changes.

Fig. 22 36

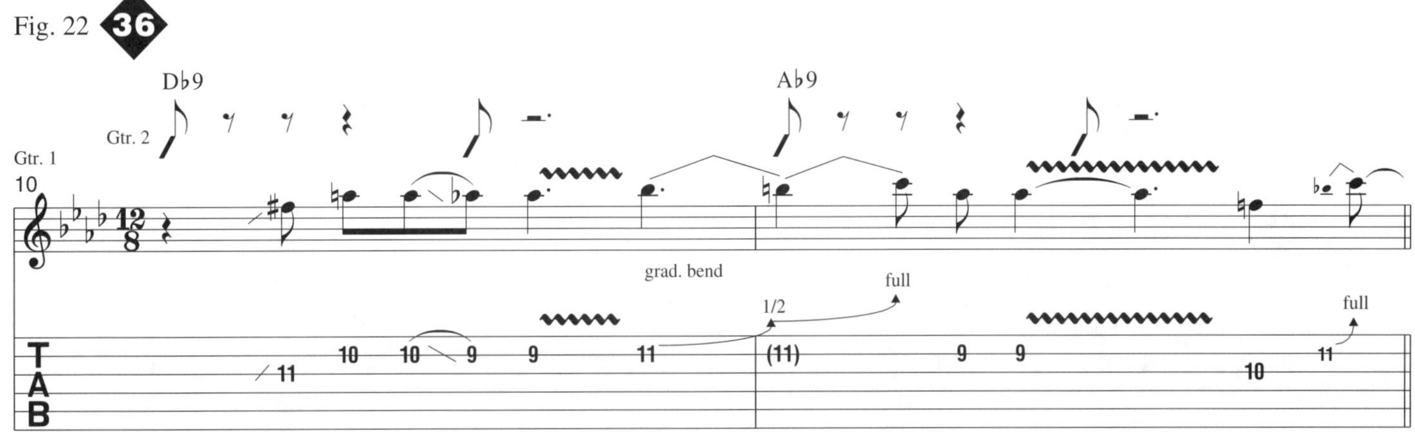

Figure 23 - Tension Lick

By the third chorus, Buddy is "just teasin'" us with musical tension by his note selection. In measure 4 (I), he bends the D♭ (4th) up a full step to the 5th (E♭), followed by the 4th, ♭3rd (C♭), root (A♭), and C♭ bent a full step across the bar line to the root (D♭) of the IV chord. He then ends the measure with the C♭ (♭7th), A♭ (5th), and G♭ (4th) bent to A♭ (5th). Notice that besides the major 3rd (C) over the I chord, Buddy relies heavily on the 4th to build tension and excitement throughout the song.

Fig. 23 37

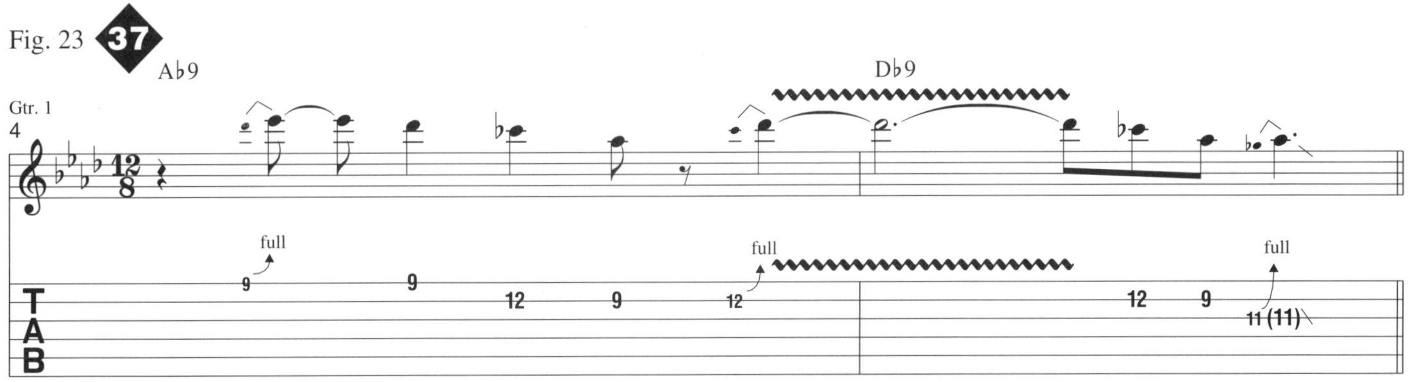

Figure 24 - ♭5th Lick

Measure 6 (IV chord) of the fifth chorus has Buddy emphasizing the ♭5th (G) more prominently than most blues guitarists would ever think of doing. He does resolve down to the root (D♭) via the ♭5th, 3rd (F), and 9th (E♭), but the ear-twitching sound of that hip ♭5th hangs in the air like the smoke from a firecracker.

Fig. 24 38

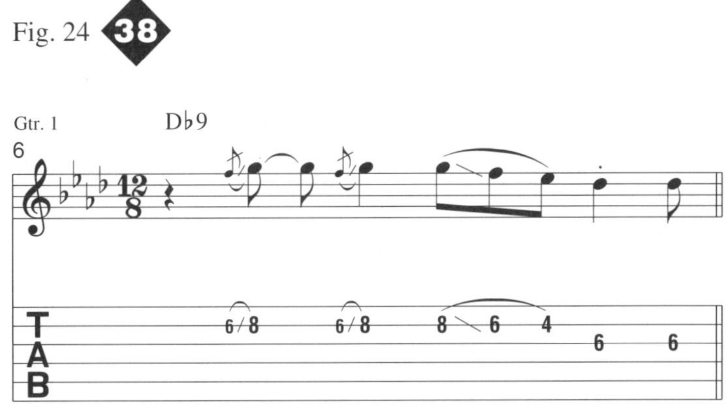

Figure 25 - Lick over I chord

Using the root (A♭) note as the anchor for these three measures (I chord) in the sixth chorus, Buddy dives off from the ♭3rd (C♭) to the major 3rd (C) on the high E string in measure 1. In measures 2 and 3, he bends up to the blue note in between the ♭3rd and 3rd. He also goes back and forth between the ♭3rd and 4th (D♭) in measure 3.

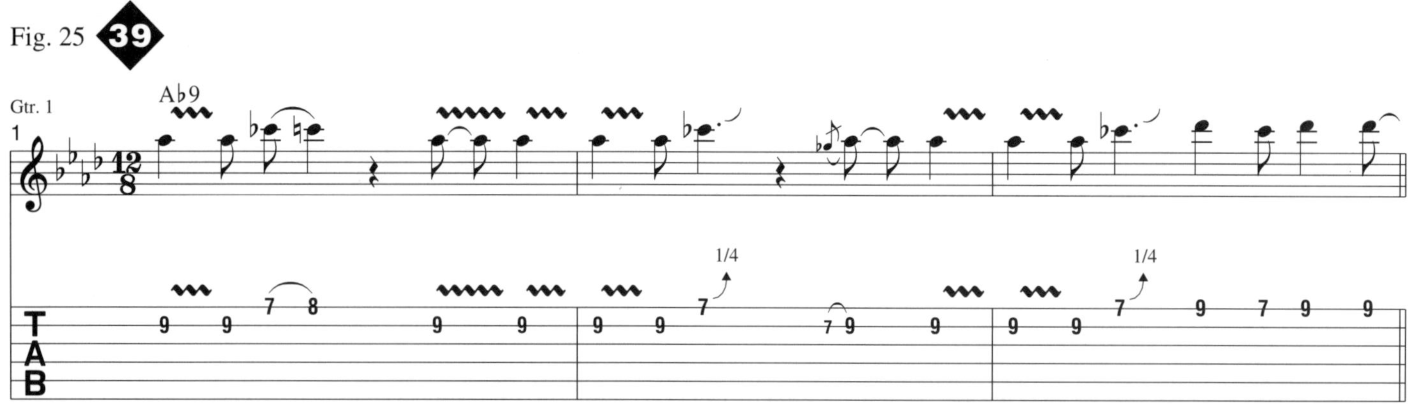

Figure 26 - Bending Lick

In the seventh chorus, Buddy connects the I (A♭) and IV (D♭) chords in measures 4 and 5 with a peppery bend of D♭ (4th) to E♭ (5th) and then down a half step to the groovy ♭5th (E♭♭). By beat 4 of the measure, he has released the bend all the way down to D♭, which he runs into measure 5. Pulling off to the ♭7th (C♭), he continues down the root position (octave) of the A♭ minor pentatonic scale, landing on the A♭ (5th) note with conviction and vibrato. He ends the measure with a quarter-step bend to the blue note in between the ♭7th and major 7th (C).

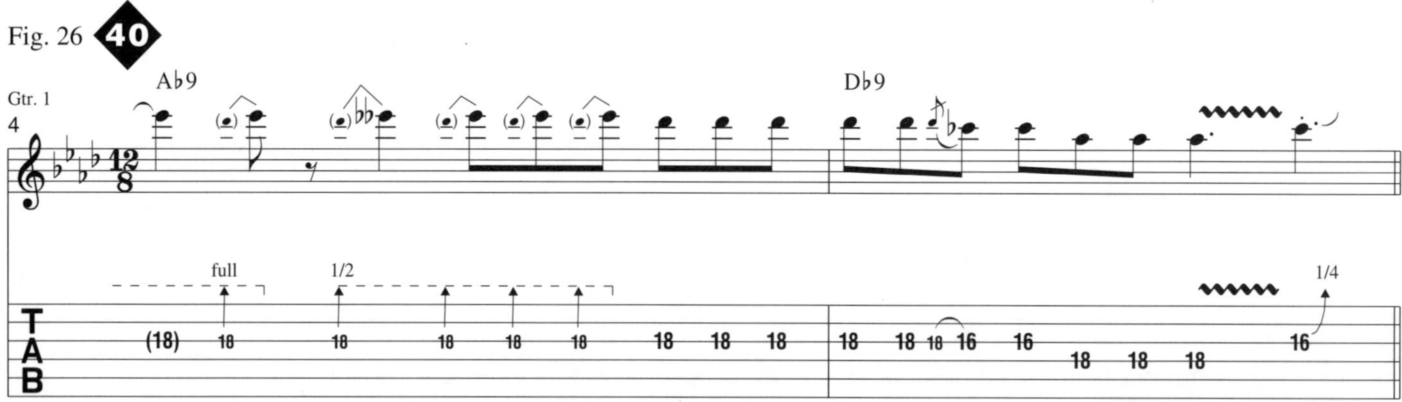

Figure 27 - Double Stop Bending Lick

Here is one that will tickle your musical funny bone. In measure 2 (I chord) of the eighth chorus, Buddy bends the ♭7th (G♭) a full step to the root (A♭) at fret 19. He then follows this classic I chord lick with a double-stop, double-string bend of the ♭5th (D) to the 5th (E♭) combined with the ♭7th bent a full step up to the root. Struck dead on, this interval is stable and consonant. Bent and vibratoed, as described, and you feel the ground shift perceptibly under your feet. Yeow!

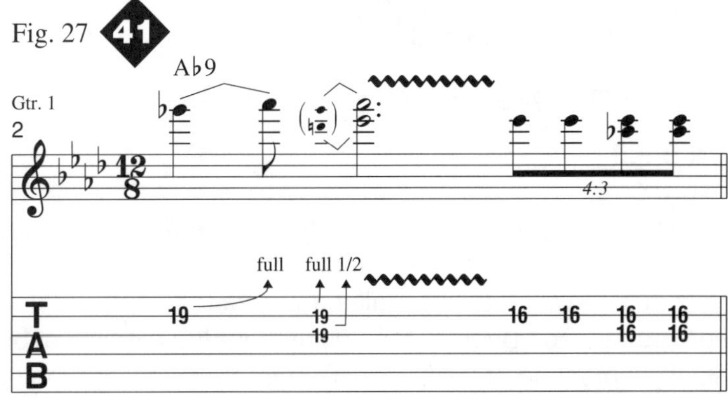

Figure 28 - Another Bending Lick

In measure 6 (IV chord) of the same chorus, Buddy pours it on. With his pinky on the 4th (G♭) at fret 19, he repeatedly bends the root (D♭) up a full step with his ring finger to the 9th (E♭). He continues with this lick for the next two measures (I chord), taking a break over the V (E♭) chord in measure 9 and repeating it again over the IV (D♭) chord in measure 10 (not shown).

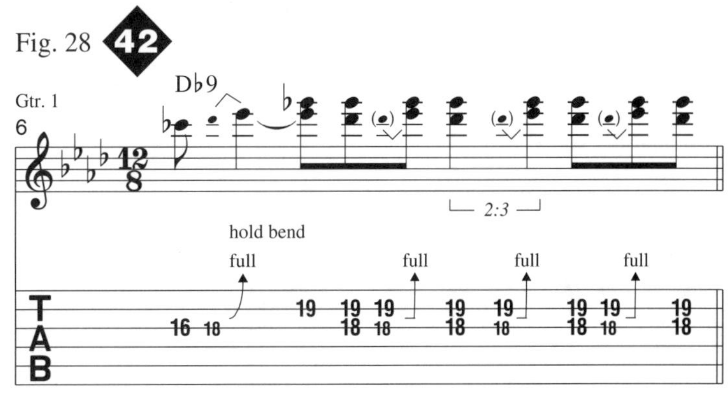

Figure 29 - Unusual Lick

With the pickup and first two measures of the ninth chorus, Buddy outdoes himself. Starting with the 9th (F) over the V (E♭) chord of the preceding chorus, he plays the 9th (B♭) of the I chord (A♭) followed by the *major 7th* (G)! He then bends the root a full step to the 9th. Ah, but the best is yet to come. After smacking the A♭/E♭ (root and 5th) dyad at the end of beat 4 in measure 1, he slides from A♭/E♭ to B♭♭/F♭ (♭9th and ♯5th) and holds it for a beat before glissing down and off the fingerboard. Frankly, this may be a mistake, but what a doozy. *Anything* sounds like resolution after that wild double stop.

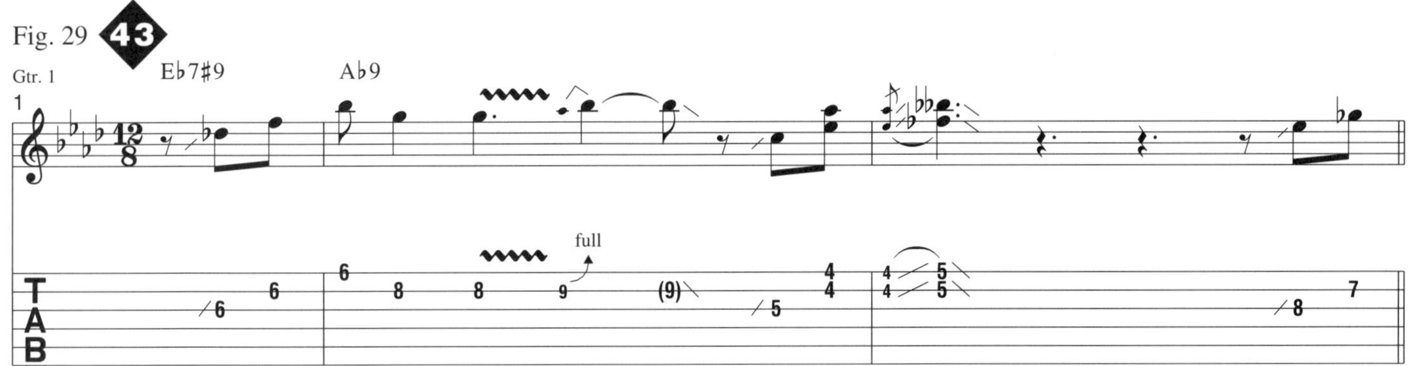

FIVE LONG YEARS

(Damn Right, I've Got the Blues)

Words and Music by Eddie Boyd

In 1991 Buddy signed on with Silvertone Records and began the next and most successful phase of his career. The title of the first release with Silvertone says it all, though at this point in time he was probably "crying the blues" all the way to the bank!

What goes around comes around, and Buddy's recordings from the nineties show a definite rock influence, especially the sound of his guitar. "Five Long Years," though, has that luscious, liquid, out-of-phase Strat tone displayed all over *A Man and the Blues*.

Figure 30 - Double-String Bend

This long, *slow* (50 bpm) blues is laden with choice fills. In measure 8 (I chord), just before the V chord, Buddy plays a fluid double-stop, double-string bend in the root position C blues box at fret 8. With his ring finger on string 3 and his pinky on string 2, he bends B♭/F (♭7th and 4th) up a half step to C♭/G♭ (*major 7th* and ♭5th), releases, and ends on the salty ♭3rd (E♭). This type of bend gives the feeling that time is suspended briefly, intensifying the strong, gravitational pull that follows with resolution to the I chord in measure 11.

Fig. 30 44

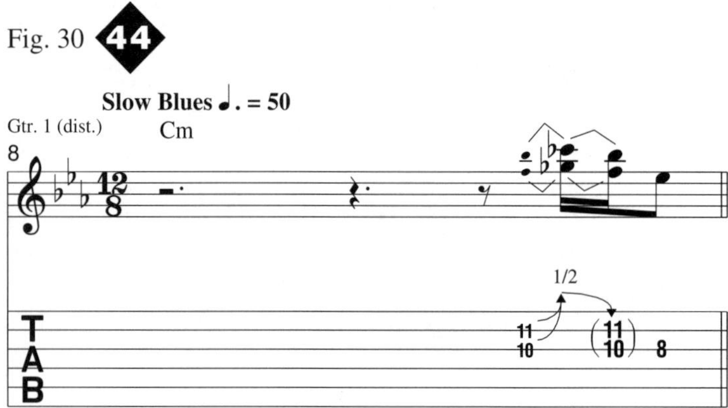

Figure 31 - Wide Bend

At the end of measure 4 (I chord), just before the change to the IV chord, Buddy leans on one of his famous 2 ½ step bends. Using his pinky, he bends the B♭ (♭7th) up to the E♭ (♭3rd), releases, and re-bends one full step to the root (C) before dropping to the 5th (G) with his index finger, followed by the 4th (F) pulled off to the ♭3rd (E♭). Like Fig. 30, this riff momentarily freezes time as it glides ahead relentlessly.

Fig. 31 45

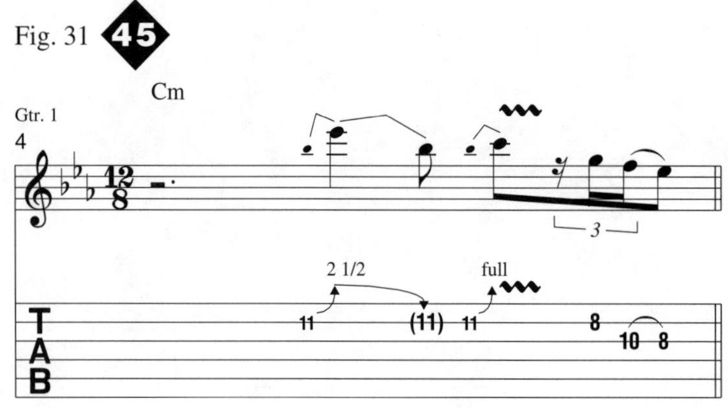

Figure 32 - Lick using the Fourth Blues "Box"

In measures 7 and 8 (I chord) of the last verse, Buddy wrings a mind-boggling, virtuosic phrase out of his tortured Strat. Toiling mightily out of the octave fourth box (pattern 4, between frets 15 and 18), he repeatedly bends the 4th (F) to the 5th (G), with regular resolution to the root (C). Interspersed along the way is a head-shaking double-stop, double-string bend of F/D♭ (4th and ♭9th) to G/E♭ (5th and ♭3rd) and the zingy ♭3rd (E♭).

You have several fingering options this high on the neck. One good system to follow is to use your pinky at fret 18, your middle finger at fret 16, and your ring finger at fret 17. For the double-string bend, this translates into your ring finger on string 3 and your pinky on string 2 at fret 18.

Check out how Buddy returns from the "Strat"-osphere at the end of this phrase by landing back in the root position at fret 8 with the F, E♭, and B♭ notes. Though his note selection here is fairly conservative, the reckless abandon with which he mashes them together creates intense musical tension that is released by the chord change to the V in measure 9.

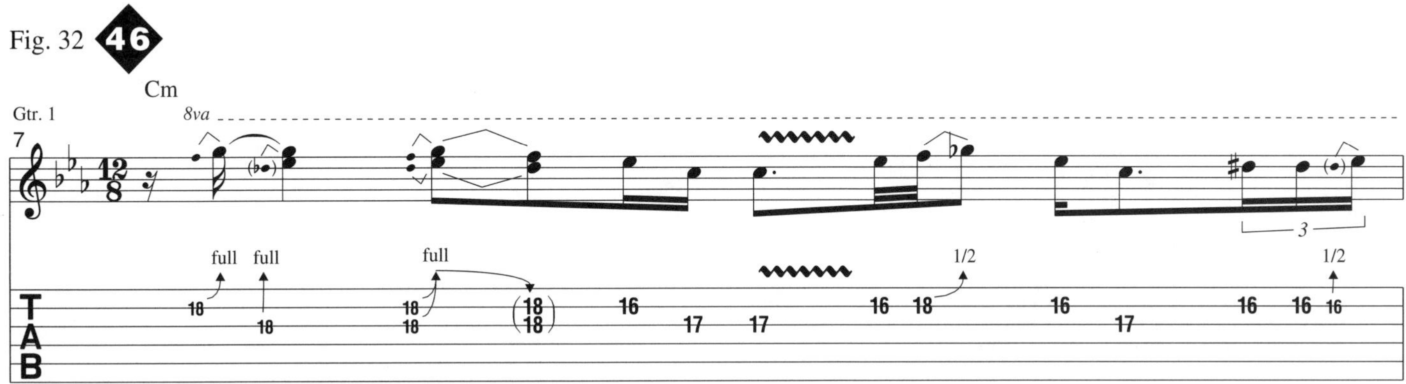

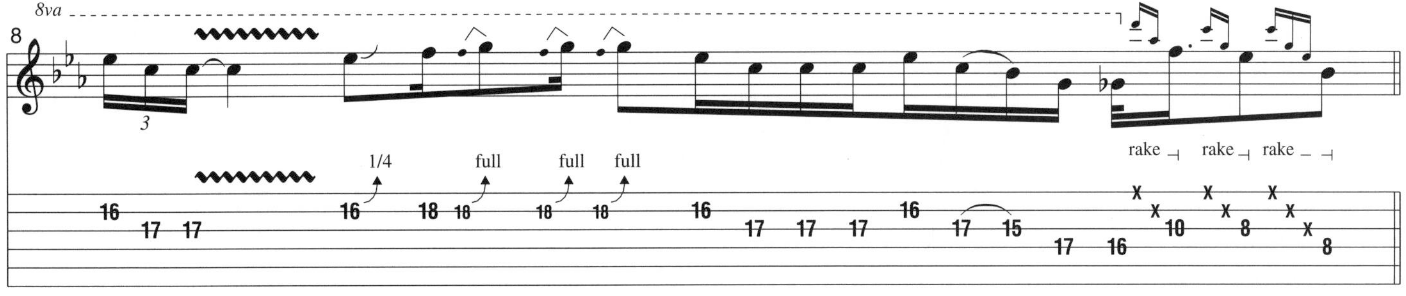

Guitar Notation Legend

Guitar Music can be notated three different ways: on a *musical staff*, in *tablature*, and in *rhythm slashes.*

RHYTHM SLASHES are written above the staff. Strum chords in the rhythm indicated. Use the chord diagrams found at the top of the first page of the transcription for the appropriate chord voicings. Round noteheads indicate single notes.

THE MUSICAL STAFF shows pitches and rhythms and is divided by bar lines into measures. Pitches are named after the first seven letters of the alphabet.

TABLATURE graphically represents the guitar fingerboard. Each horizontal line represents a a string, and each number represents a fret.

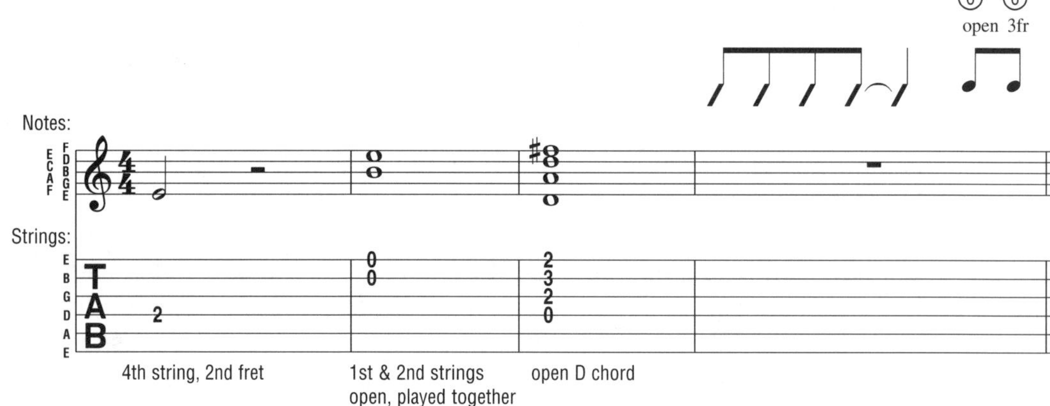

Definitions for Special Guitar Notation

HALF-STEP BEND: Strike the note and bend up 1/2 step.

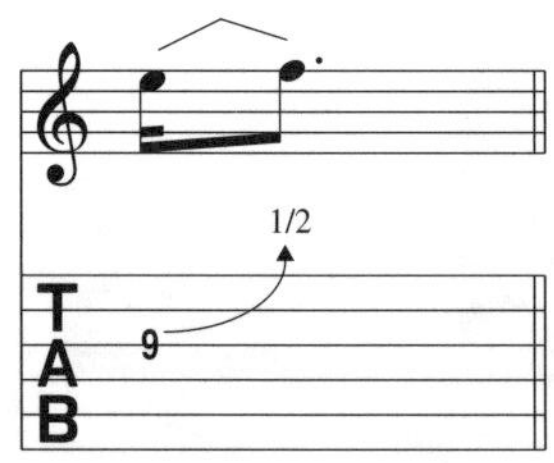

WHOLE-STEP BEND: Strike the note and bend up one step.

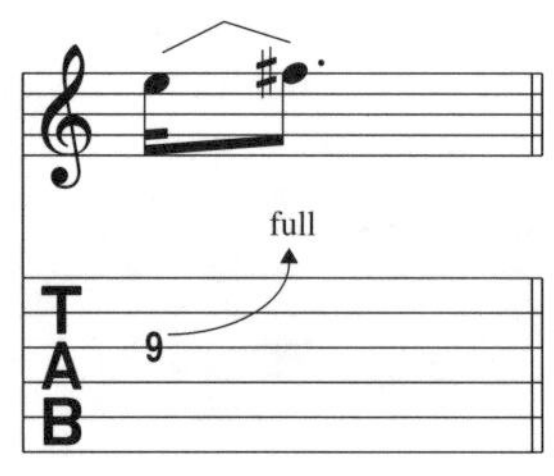

GRACE NOTE BEND: Strike the note and bend up as indicated. The first note does not take up any time.

SLIGHT (MICROTONE) BEND: Strike the note and bend up 1/4 step.

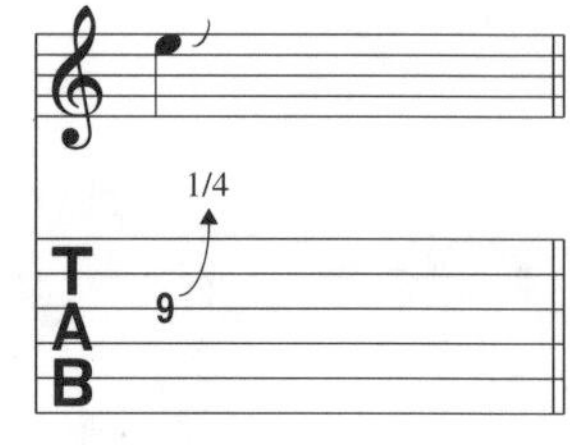

BEND AND RELEASE: Strike the note and bend up as indicated, then release back to the original note. Only the first note is struck.

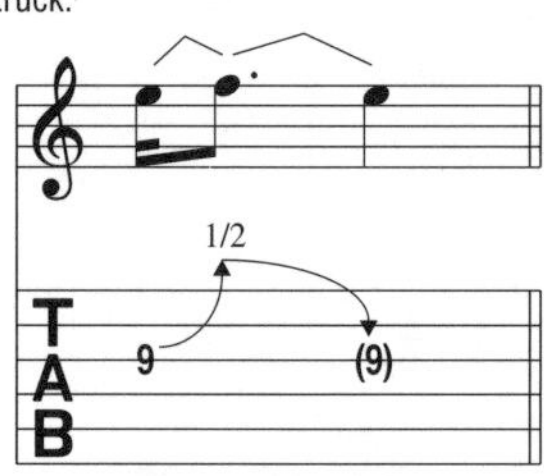

PRE-BEND: Bend the note as indicated, then strike it.

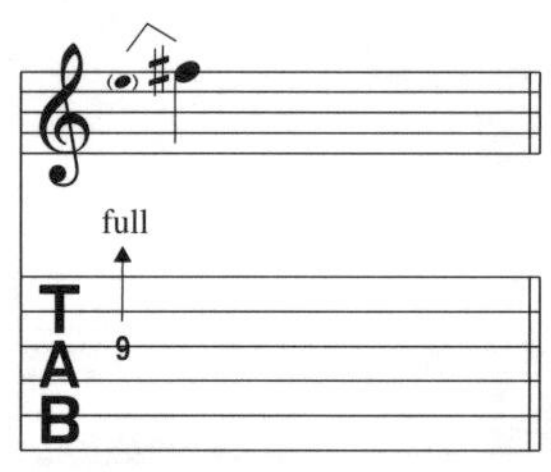

PRE-BEND AND RELEASE: Bend the note as indicated. Strike it and release the bend back to the original note.

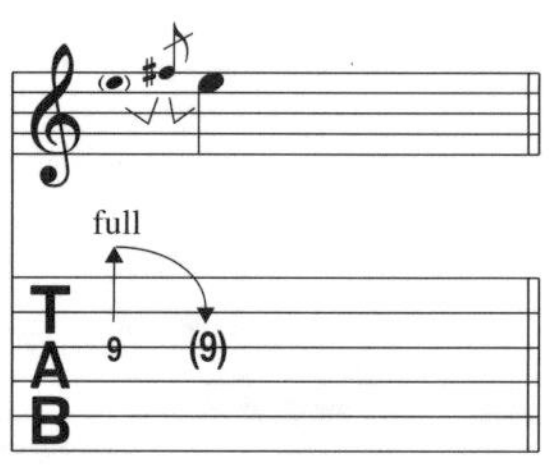

UNISON BEND: Strike the two notes simultaneously and bend the lower note up to the pitch of the higher.

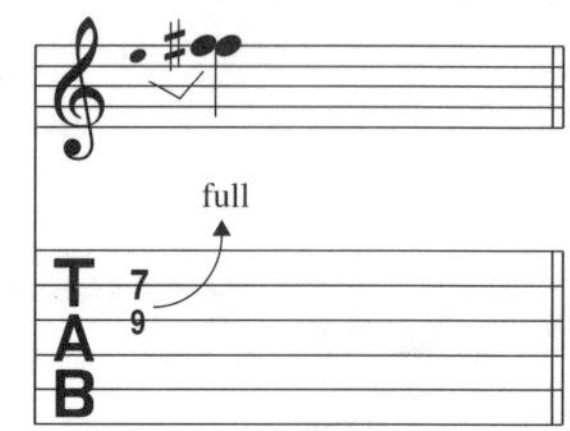

VIBRATO: The string is vibrated by rapidly bending and releasing the note with the fretting hand.

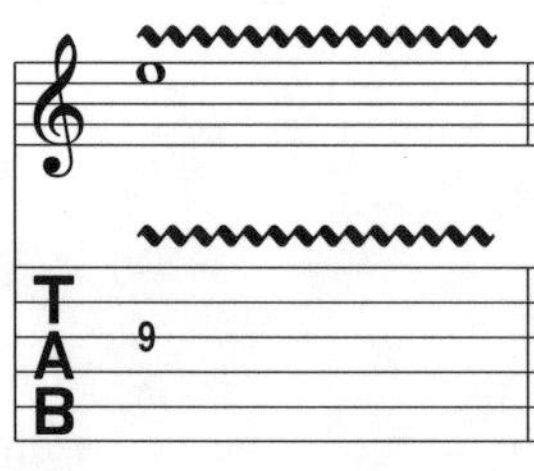

WIDE VIBRATO: The pitch is varied to a greater degree by vibrating with the fretting hand.

HAMMER-ON: Strike the first (lower) note with one finger, then sound the higher note (on the same string) with another finger by fretting it without picking.

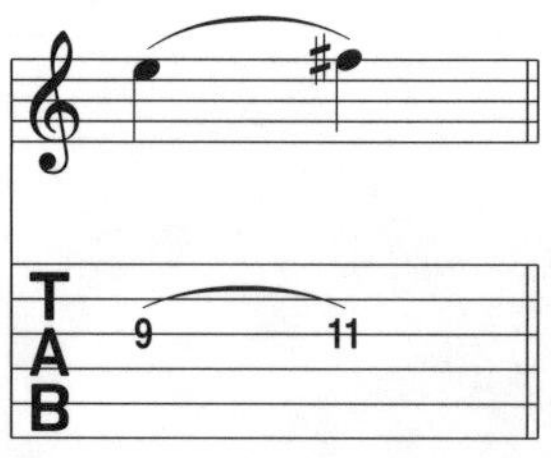

PULL-OFF: Place both fingers on the notes to be sounded. Strike the first note and without picking, pull the finger off to sound the second (lower) note.

LEGATO SLIDE: Strike the first note and then slide the same fret-hand finger up or down to the second note. The second note is not struck.

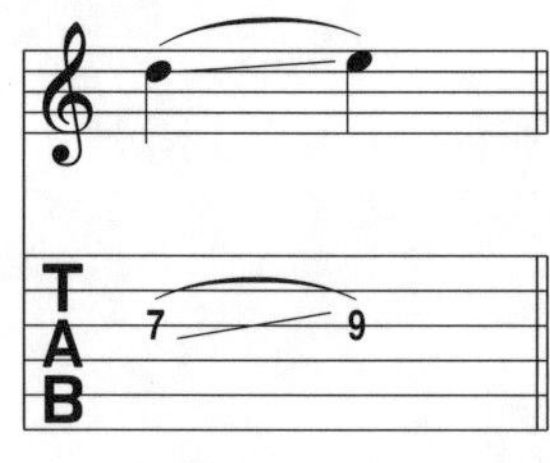

SHIFT SLIDE: Same as legato slide, except the second note is struck.

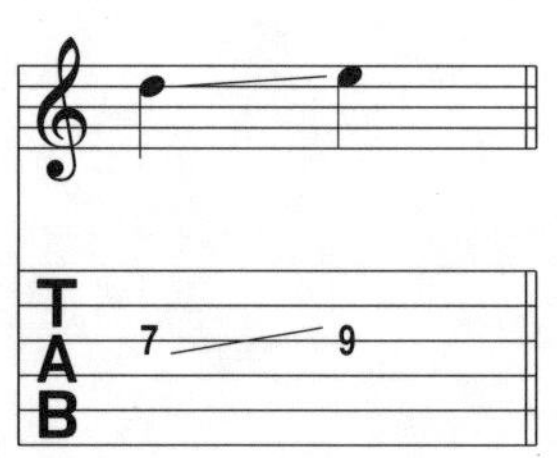

TRILL: Very rapidly alternate between the notes indicated by continuously hammering on and pulling off.

TAPPING: Hammer ("tap") the fret indicated with the pick-hand index or middle finger and pull off to the note fretted by the fret hand.

NATURAL HARMONIC: Strike the note while the fret-hand lightly touches the string directly over the fret indicated.

PINCH HARMONIC: The note is fretted normally and a harmonic is produced by adding the edge of the thumb or the tip of the index finger of the pick hand to the normal pick attack.

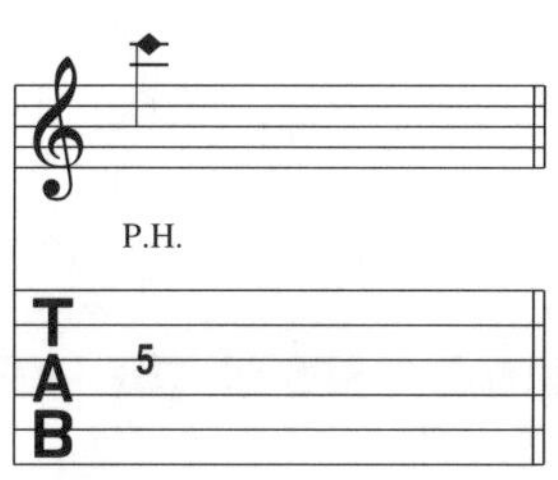

HARP HARMONIC: The note is fretted normally and a harmonic is produced by gently resting the pick hand's index finger directly above the indicated fret (in parentheses) while the pick hand's thumb or pick assists by plucking the appropriate string.

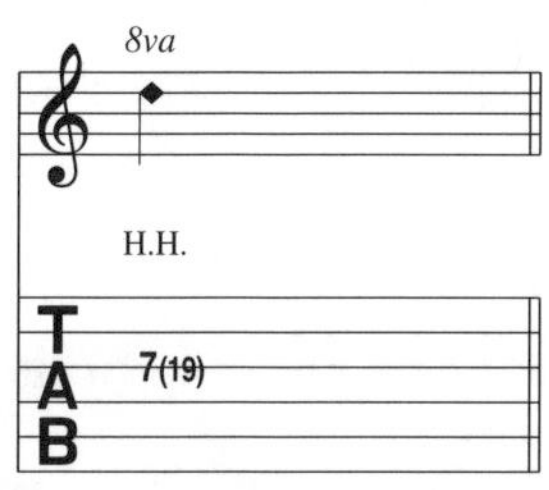

PICK SCRAPE: The edge of the pick is rubbed down (or up) the string, producing a scratchy sound.

MUFFLED STRINGS: A percussive sound is produced by laying the fret hand across the string(s) without depressing, and striking them with the pick hand.

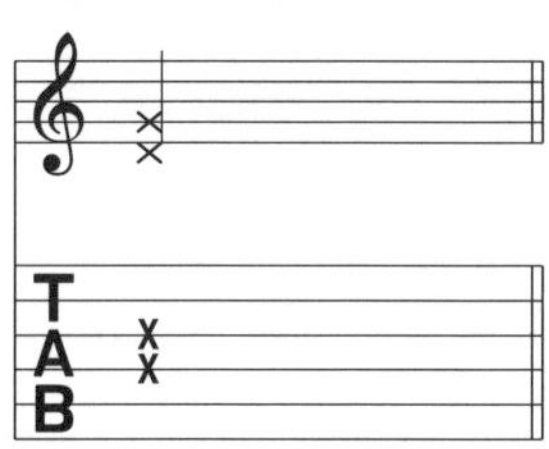

PALM MUTING: The note is partially muted by the pick hand lightly touching the string(s) just before the bridge.

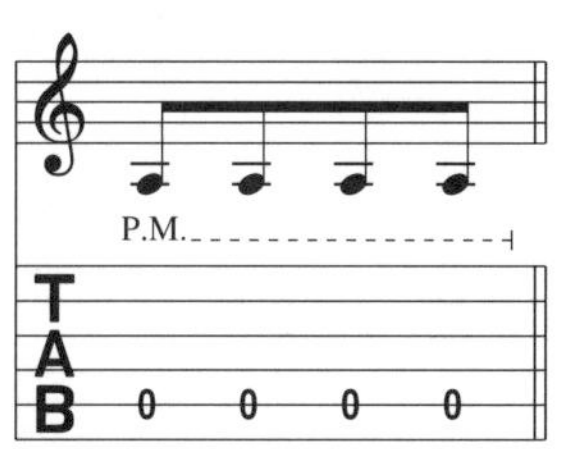

RAKE: Drag the pick across the strings indicated with a single motion.

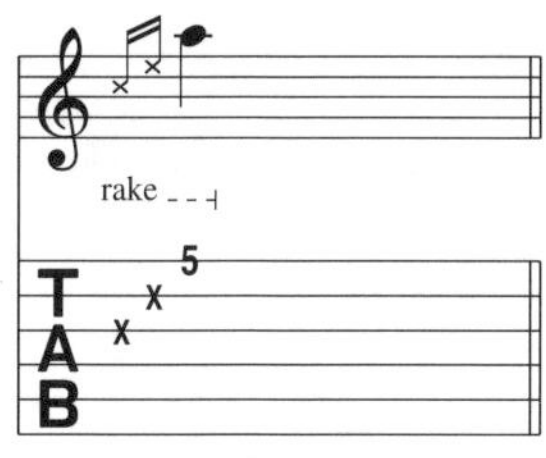

TREMOLO PICKING: The note is picked as rapidly and continuously as possible.

ARPEGGIATE: Play the notes of the chord indicated by quickly rolling them from bottom to top.

VIBRATO BAR DIVE AND RETURN: The pitch of the note or chord is dropped a specified number of steps (in rhythm) then returned to the original pitch.

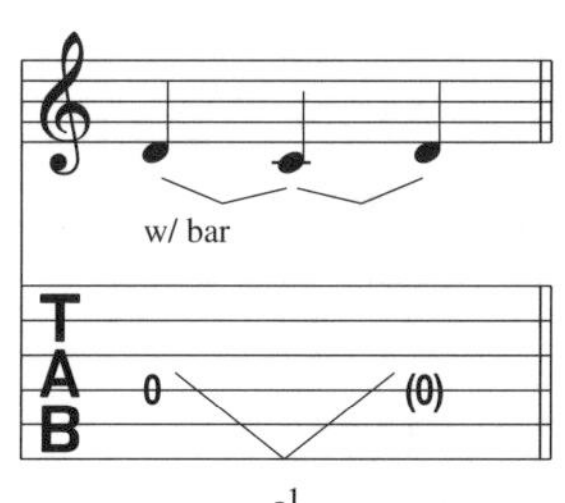

VIBRATO BAR SCOOP: Depress the bar just before striking the note, then quickly release the bar.

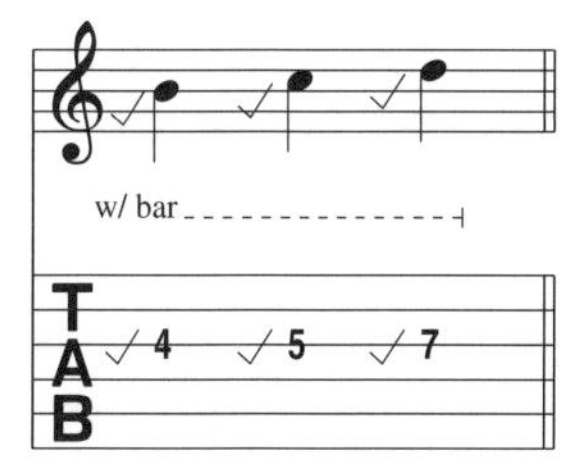

VIBRATO BAR DIP: Strike the note and then immediately drop a specified number of steps, then release back to the original pitch.

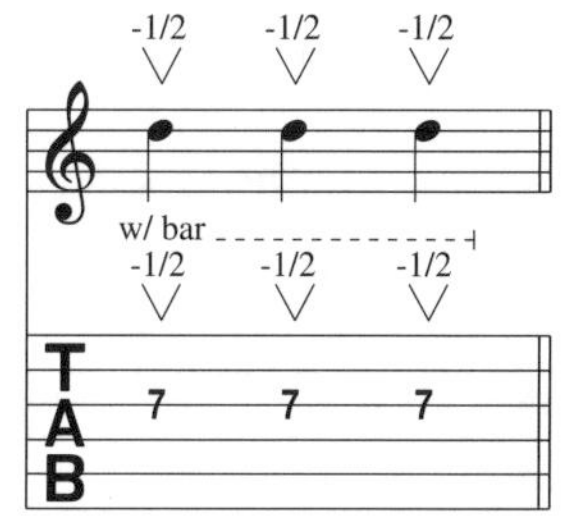

Additional Musical Definitions

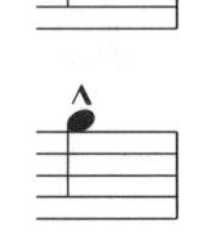 *(accent)* • Accentuate note (play it louder)

 *(accent)* • Accentuate note with great intensity

 *(staccato)* • Play the note short

⊓ • Downstroke

V • Upstroke

D.S. al Coda • Go back to the sign (𝄋), then play until the measure marked "***To Coda***," then skip to the section labelled "***Coda***."

D.S. al Fine • Go back to the beginning of the song and play until the measure marked "***Fine***" (end).

Rhy. Fig. • Label used to recall a recurring accompaniment pattern (usually chordal).

Riff • Label used to recall composed, melodic lines (usually single notes) which recur.

Fill • Label used to identify a brief melodic figure which is to be inserted into the arrangement.

Rhy. Fill • A chordal version of a Fill.

tacet • Instrument is silent (drops out).

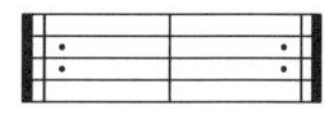 • Repeat measures between signs.

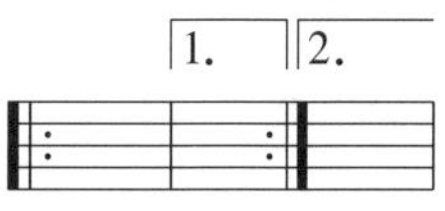

• When a repeated section has different endings, play the first ending only the first time and the second ending only the second time.

NOTE: Tablature numbers in parentheses mean:
1. The note is being sustained over a system (note in standard notation is tied), or
2. The note is sustained, but a new articulation (such as a hammer-on, pull-off, slide or vibrato begins, or
3. The note is a barely audible "ghost" note (note in standard notation is also in parentheses).

GUITAR *signature licks*®

The Signature Licks book/audio packs are especially formatted to give guitarists instruction on how to play a particular artist style by using the actual transcribed, "right from the record" licks! Designed for use by anyone from beginner right up to the experienced player who is looking to expand their insight. The books contain full performance notes and an overview of each artist or group's style with transcriptions in notes and tab. The audio features full-demo playing tips and techniques, as well as playing examples at a slower tempo.

ACOUSTIC GUITAR OF '60S AND '70S
by Wolf Marshall
00695024 Book/CD Pack $19.95

ACOUSTIC GUITAR OF '80S AND '90S
by Wolf Marshall
00695033 Book/CD Pack $19.95

AEROSMITH 1973-1979
by Wolf Marshall
00695106 Book/CD Pack $19.95

AEROSMITH 1979-1998
by Wolf Marshall
00695219 Book/CD Pack $19.95

BEATLES BASS
by Wolf Marshall
00695283 Book/CD Pack $17.95

THE BEATLES FAVORITES
by Wolf Marshall
00695096 Book/CD Pack $19.95

THE BEATLES HITS
by Wolf Marshall
00695049 Book/CD Pack $19.95

THE BEST OF BLACK SABBATH
by Troy Stetina
00695249 Book/CD Pack $19.95

BLUES GUITAR CLASSICS
by Wolf Marshall
00695177 Book/CD Pack $17.95

THE BEST OF ERIC CLAPTON
by Jeff Perrin
00695038 Book/CD Pack $19.95

ERIC CLAPTON – THE BLUESMAN
by Andy Aledort
00695040 Book/CD Pack $19.95

ERIC CLAPTON – FROM THE ALBUM UNPLUGGED
by Wolf Marshall
00695250 Book/CD Pack $19.95

THE BEST OF CREAM
by Wolf Marshall
00695251 Book/CD Pack $19.95

THE BEST OF DEF LEPPARD
by Jeff Perrin
00696516 Book/CD Pack $19.95

GREATEST GUITAR SOLOS OF ALL TIME
by Wolf Marshall
00695301 Book/CD Pack $17.95

GUITAR INSTRUMENTAL HITS
by Wolf Marshall
00695309 Book/CD Pack $16.95

GUITAR RIFFS OF THE '60S
by Wolf Marshall
00695218 Book/CD pack $16.95

GUITAR RIFFS OF THE '70S
by Wolf Marshall
00695158 Book/CD Pack $16.95

THE BEST OF GUNS N' ROSES
by Jeff Perrin
00695183 Book/CD Pack $19.95

JIMI HENDRIX
by Andy Aledort
00696560 Book/CD Pack $19.95

ERIC JOHNSON
by Wolf Marshall
00699317 Book/CD Pack $19.95

THE BEST OF KISS
by Jeff Perrin
00699413 Book/CD Pack $19.95

MARK KNOPFLER
by Wolf Marshall
00695178 Book/CD Pack $19.95

MEGADETH
by Jeff Perrin
00695041 Book/CD Pack $19.95

THE GUITARS OF ELVIS
by Wolf Marshall
00696507 Book/CD Pack $19.95

BEST OF QUEEN
by Wolf Marshall
00695097 Book/CD Pack $19.95

THE RED HOT CHILI PEPPERS
by Dale Turner
00695173 Book/CD Pack $19.95

THE ROLLING STONES
by Wolf Marshall
00695079 Book/CD Pack $19.95

BEST OF CARLOS SANTANA
by Wolf Marshall
00695010 Book/CD Pack $19.95

THE BEST OF JOE SATRIANI
by Dale Turner
00695216 Book/CD Pack $19.95

STEVE VAI
by Jeff Perrin
00673247 Book/CD Pack $22.95

STEVE VAI – ALIEN LOVE SECRETS: THE NAKED VAMPS
00695223 Book/CD Pack $19.95

STEVE VAI – FIRE GARDEN: THE NAKED VAMPS
00695166 Book/CD Pack $19.95

STEVIE RAY VAUGHAN
by Wolf Marshall
00699316 Book/CD Pack $19.95

THE GUITAR STYLE OF STEVIE RAY VAUGHAN
by Wolf Marshall
00695155 Book/CD Pack $19.95

FOR MORE INFORMATION, SEE YOUR LOCAL MUSIC DEALER, OR WRITE TO:

HAL•LEONARD® CORPORATION

7777 W. BLUEMOUND RD. P.O. BOX 13819 MILWAUKEE, WI 53213

Prices, contents and availability subject to change without notice.